PROVEN STRATEGIES FOR BUSINESS GROWTH AND PROFIT

BY

MUJAHID BAKHT

Hardcover: ISBN 978-1-961299-08-5

Paperback: ISBN 978-1-961299-09-2

EBook : ISBN 978-1-961299-10-8

Published by

Atlas Amazon LLC

United States of America

TABLE OF CONTENTS

ABOUT AUTHER

LIFE HISTORY Mr. Bakht is a mature, experienced, extremely enthusiastic, energetic, administrator, and thirty-six years have proven experience as a businessman in international marketing and public relations. Mr. Bakht is an International Real Estate Specialist, and Professional Business and Projects Consultant. He was born in Pakistan, Educated in Pakistan and USA. Presently American Citizen belongs to a business-oriented family. Thirty-Six years Resident of New York, USA.

BUSINESS HISTORY: Mr. Bakht is a Founder & President of Atlas Amazon, LLC., Mr. Bakht is a business developer and multilingual business specialist in the Caribbean, South East Asia, and the Middle East emerging markets Mr. Bakht has served, met, and host many heads of the States. Also, maintain a close relationship with investors of high net worth in the USA.

CAREER: Mr. Bakht has been engaged with many multinational companies in the field of international real estate investment, communication, technology, diamond, gold, mining, Pre-Feb housing, wind & solar energy, outsourcing management, and project consulting along with business partners & associates worldwide. Mr. Bakht has participated in major national and international conferences including participated in United Nations (U.N.O.) conferences.

TRAVEL: Mr. Bakht is well-traveled and has visited many countries worldwide.

MANAGEMENT EXPERIENCE: Thirty-Six years of diversified experience in project consulting, marketing, and business management. As a Director of Marketing, Director of Public Relations, Director of International Affairs, Executive Vice President, President, CEO, and Chairman of many national & multinational companies. Mr. Bakht hired and trained many professionals as business consultants in international marketing and supervised them.

CERTIFICATE OF ACHIEVEMENT: Achievement Award was presented to Mr. Bakht by Stephen Fossler for five years of continued growth and customer satisfaction from 1996-to 2001.

HONORS MEMBER: Madison Who's Who of Professionals, having demonstrated exemplary achievement and distinguished contributions to the business community, registered at the Library of Congress in Washington D.C. USA. (2007 & 2008)

HONORS MEMBER: Premiere who's Who International, professional business executive having demonstrated exemplary achievement and distinguished contributions to the International business community, 2008 and 2009.

CERTIFICATES: Certificate of Authenticity from Bill Rodham Clinton, President of the United States, and Hillary Rodham Clinton First Lady, USA. (July 20, 2000);

CERTIFICATE OF AUTHENTICITY: from Terence R. McAuliffe, Chairman of Democratic National Committee, Tom Dachle, Senate Democratic Leader, Dick Gephardt, House Democratic Leader, USA. (June 16, 2001);

CERTIFICATE OF AUTHENTICITY: from Terence R. McAuliffe, Chairman of Democratic National Committee, USA. (April 16, 2002).

CHAPTER 1

IDENTIFYING YOUR BUSINESS GROWTH GOALS

To succeed in the competitive business landscape, it is crucial for entrepreneurs to have a comprehensive understanding of their business's current position. This involves evaluating various aspects of the organization, including its financial performance, market share, competitive advantage, and operational efficiency. By assessing the current position, businesses can identify areas of strength and weakness, which ultimately helps in crafting effective growth strategies. In this 3000-word discussion, we will explore various factors and methods to evaluate your business's current position.

Financial Performance

The first step in understanding your business's current position is to evaluate its financial performance. This involves reviewing financial statements, such as the balance sheet, income statement, and cash flow statement. These documents provide valuable insights into the company's profitability, liquidity, solvency, and overall financial health.

Key financial ratios, including gross margin, net profit margin, return on assets (ROA), and return on equity (ROE), should be calculated and compared to industry benchmarks to determine your business's financial standing. By analyzing financial performance, businesses can identify trends, areas of concern, and opportunities for improvement.

Market Share

Market share is a crucial indicator of a business's current position within its industry. To calculate market share, divide your company's total sales by the total sales of the industry. This metric provides insight into your business's competitiveness and relative standing within the market.

A growing market share indicates that your business is capturing a larger portion of the market, while a declining share may signal the need for improved marketing, product offerings, or customer service. Comparing your market share to that of your competitors can provide valuable insights into your business's strengths and areas for improvement.

Competitive Advantage

Understanding your business's competitive advantage is key to evaluating its current position. A competitive advantage is a unique attribute or characteristic that sets your company apart from others in the market, allowing you to outperform competitors. This advantage can come in various forms, such as superior product quality, exceptional customer service, or an efficient supply chain.

To assess your competitive advantage, identify the factors that set your business apart from its competitors and evaluate how well these factors are being leveraged. A strong competitive advantage is essential for long-term success and growth, as it enables your business to capture market share and sustain profitability.

Operational Efficiency

Assessing your business's operational efficiency is vital in understanding its current position. Operational efficiency refers to the effectiveness with which a company utilizes its resources, including labor, capital, and raw materials, to produce goods and services. Higher operational efficiency typically results in lower costs and increased profitability.

Key performance indicators (KPIs) can be used to measure operational efficiency, such as inventory turnover, labor productivity, and asset utilization. By comparing your business's KPIs to industry benchmarks, you can identify areas where your operations are excelling or falling short. Continuous improvement in operational efficiency is crucial for maintaining a competitive edge and driving business growth.

Customer Satisfaction

Customer satisfaction is a critical aspect of evaluating your business's current position, as it directly impacts customer loyalty, word-of-mouth marketing, and overall revenue.

Conducting customer satisfaction surveys and monitoring customer reviews and feedback on social media and review websites can help you gauge your business's performance in meeting customer expectations.

Identifying areas where customers are consistently dissatisfied or noting recurring complaints can help you address these issues and improve the overall customer experience. A business with high customer satisfaction is more likely to retain its existing customer base and attract new customers, driving growth and profitability.

Employee Engagement and Satisfaction

Your employees play a crucial role in determining your business's current position. Engaged and satisfied employees are more likely to be productive, contribute innovative ideas, and provide excellent customer service. Conversely, low employee engagement and satisfaction can lead to high turnover rates, decreased productivity, and a negative impact on your business's performance.

To assess employee engagement and satisfaction, consider conducting regular employee surveys or creating open channels for feedback. These measures can help identify areas where employees feel unsupported, unappreciated, or overworked. Addressing these concerns and fostering a positive work environment can enhance employee engagement, which in turn can contribute to improved business performance.

Market Trends and Industry Dynamics

Understanding your business's current position also requires a comprehensive analysis of market trends and industry dynamics. This involves researching and monitoring industry news, reports, and studies to identify emerging trends, technological advancements, and shifts in consumer behavior that could affect your business.

By staying abreast of market trends and industry developments, you can identify opportunities for growth, such as the introduction of new products or services, or the expansion into new markets. Moreover, understanding industry dynamics can help you anticipate potential threats, such as increased competition or regulatory changes, and develop strategies to mitigate these risks.

SWOT Analysis

A SWOT (Strengths, Weaknesses, Opportunities, and Threats) analysis is a valuable tool for understanding your business's current position. By examining the internal strengths and weaknesses of your organization and the external opportunities and threats in the market, you can gain a comprehensive view of your business's strategic landscape.

Strengths: Identify the unique capabilities, resources, and characteristics that give your business a competitive edge. These may include a highly skilled workforce, a strong brand reputation, or proprietary technology.

Weaknesses: Recognize the areas where your business is underperforming or lacks resources compared to competitors. This may include outdated technology, high employee turnover, or a limited product range.

Opportunities: Look for external factors or market trends that present growth opportunities for your business, such as an underserved market segment, emerging technologies, or changes in consumer preferences.

Threats: Identify external risks or challenges that could negatively impact your business, such as increased competition, economic downturns, or regulatory changes.

The SWOT analysis helps businesses identify areas for improvement, capitalize on opportunities, and develop strategies to mitigate threats, thereby providing a clear roadmap for growth and success.

Benchmarking

Benchmarking involves comparing your business's performance metrics with those of your competitors or industry leaders. This process allows you to evaluate your business's current position relative to others in the market and identify best practices that can be implemented to improve performance.

To conduct a benchmarking analysis, first identify the key performance indicators (KPIs) relevant to your business, such as revenue growth, customer retention rate, or operational efficiency. Next, gather data on these metrics for your competitors or industry leaders. By comparing your business's performance to that of other companies, you can identify areas where your business excels or falls short, and develop strategies for improvement.

Setting SMART Goals

Once you have a thorough understanding of your business's current position, it's essential to set SMART (Specific, Measurable, Achievable, Relevant, and Time-bound) goals for growth and improvement. These goals should be based on the insights gained from the various analyses discussed above and should focus on addressing weaknesses, capitalizing on opportunities, and mitigating threats.

By setting SMART goals, your business can develop a clear roadmap for growth, with specific targets and timelines that enable you to track progress and measure success. Regularly monitoring and adjusting these goals, based on changing market conditions and business performance, will help ensure continued growth and profitability.

Setting realistic and achievable growth targets

Setting realistic and achievable growth targets is an essential aspect of successful business planning and development. Well-defined targets provide direction and focus, motivating the entire organization to work towards common objectives. In this 3000-word guide, we will discuss various factors and methods to help you set realistic and achievable growth targets for your business.

Conduct a Comprehensive Business Analysis

Before setting growth targets, it's crucial to conduct a comprehensive analysis of your business's current position, as discussed in the previous section. Evaluating your financial performance, market share, competitive advantage, operational efficiency, customer satisfaction, employee engagement, and industry dynamics provides a solid foundation for setting realistic targets. A thorough understanding of your business's strengths, weaknesses, opportunities, and threats enables you to develop growth strategies tailored to your unique situation.

Define Clear and Specific Objectives

Vague or overly broad growth targets can be difficult to measure and achieve. Instead, set clear and specific objectives that clearly outline what you want to accomplish. These objectives should be closely aligned with your overall business vision and mission, ensuring that your growth targets support your long-term strategic goals.

For example, instead of setting a target to "increase revenue," consider a more specific objective like "increase annual revenue by 15% within the next two years by expanding into new markets and launching new products."

Use the SMART Criteria

To ensure that your growth targets are realistic and achievable, use the SMART criteria. SMART stands for Specific, Measurable, Achievable, Relevant, and Time-bound Applying the SMART framework to your growth targets ensures that they are well-defined, actionable, and trackable.

Specific: Clearly define your target, outlining the desired outcome and the steps required to achieve it.

Measurable: Establish quantifiable metrics to track progress and measure success.

Achievable: Ensure that your target is attainable, considering your business's current position, resources, and market conditions.

Relevant: Align your growth target with your overall business strategy and objectives.

Time-bound: Set a deadline for achieving your target, creating a sense of urgency and accountability.

Consider Your Business's Resources and Capabilities

Setting realistic and achievable growth targets requires a thorough understanding of your business's resources and capabilities. Assess your financial resources, human capital, technology, and infrastructure to determine whether they can support your growth objectives. If you identify gaps or limitations, consider strategies to acquire or develop the necessary resources to achieve your targets, such as raising capital, hiring additional staff, or investing in new technology.

Analyze Market Potential and Industry Trends

Understanding market potential and industry trends is crucial for setting realistic growth targets. Conduct market research and analyze industry reports to identify growth opportunities, emerging trends, and potential challenges. This information can help you set targets that are relevant and achievable within the context of the market and industry landscape.

For example, if you identify an underserved market segment with high demand for your product or service, you might set a growth target to capture a specific percentage of that market share within a defined timeframe.

Benchmark Against Competitors and Industry Leaders

Benchmarking your business against competitors and industry leaders can provide valuable insights into achievable growth targets. Analyze the growth rates and performance metrics of similar businesses to determine what is realistic and attainable within your industry. While it's important to aim high, setting growth targets that are significantly higher than industry norms without a clear plan or competitive advantage can lead to disappointment and wasted resources.

Set Short-Term and Long-Term Targets

Setting both short-term and long-term growth targets allows you to maintain focus on immediate objectives while working towards your ultimate business vision. Short-term targets (typically 1-2 years) should be specific, actionable steps that contribute to the achievement of your long-term objectives. Long-term targets (typically 3-5 years or more) represent your overarching growth aspirations and should align with your overall business strategy.

Balancing short-term and long-term targets ensures that your business remains adaptable to changing market conditions and can adjust strategies as needed to achieve sustained growth.

Involve Your Team in the Target-Setting Process

Involving your team in setting growth targets helps ensure that they are realistic and achievable. Your team members have valuable insights into the challenges and opportunities within their specific areas of responsibility and can contribute ideas and strategies for achieving growth objectives. Involving your team in the process also fosters a sense of ownership and commitment to the targets, increasing motivation and engagement.

Develop a Detailed Action Plan

Once you have set your growth targets, develop a detailed action plan outlining the steps, resources, and timelines required to achieve them. This plan should include specific strategies and initiatives, such as marketing campaigns, product development, process improvements, or organizational restructuring.

Assign responsibilities to team members and establish clear performance metrics and milestones to track progress. Regularly reviewing and updating your action plan ensures that your business remains on track to achieve its growth targets and can adjust strategies as needed.

Monitor Progress and Adjust Targets as Needed

Setting realistic and achievable growth targets is an ongoing process that requires continuous monitoring and adjustment. Regularly review your progress against your targets and performance metrics to identify areas where your business is excelling or falling short.

If you find that your growth targets are consistently not being met, consider whether they were initially too ambitious or whether there are underlying issues that need to be addressed, such as operational inefficiencies, competitive pressures, or changing market conditions. Adjust your targets and strategies as needed to ensure that they remain realistic and achievable in light of new information or circumstances.

Celebrate Achievements and Learn from Challenges

Recognizing and celebrating the achievement of growth targets is essential for maintaining motivation and momentum within your organization. Acknowledge the hard work and dedication of your team members and reward their contributions to the business's growth.

At the same time, it's important to learn from challenges and setbacks. Analyze any shortfalls in achieving your growth targets to identify areas for improvement and adjust your strategies accordingly. Embracing a growth mindset and continuously learning from both successes and challenges will help your business adapt and thrive in an ever-changing business landscape.

Maintain a Balance between Growth and Stability

While setting ambitious growth targets can drive your business forward, it's crucial to maintain a balance between growth and stability. Pursuing growth at the expense of financial stability, operational efficiency, or customer satisfaction can lead to long-term problems and undermine your business's success.

As you set and work towards your growth targets, regularly assess the impact of your growth strategies on your overall business health. Ensure that you maintain adequate cash reserves, operational efficiency, and customer satisfaction while pursuing your growth objectives.

Aligning growth goals with your company's mission and vision

A company's mission and vision are the foundation upon which its growth goals should be built. A mission statement defines the core purpose of the business and its reason for existence, while a vision statement outlines the company's long-term aspirations and desired future state. Aligning growth goals with your company's mission and vision ensures that your business remains focused on its fundamental objectives and values, while pursuing expansion and increased profitability. In this 3000-word guide, we will discuss the steps and strategies for aligning your growth goals with your company's mission and vision.

Revisit and Reaffirm Your Company's Mission and Vision

Before setting growth goals, take the time to revisit and reaffirm your company's mission and vision statements. Ensure that these statements accurately reflect your business's core purpose, values, and long-term aspirations. If necessary, revise your mission and vision to ensure they are current, clear, and compelling.

Engaging your team in this process can help build a shared understanding and commitment to your company's mission and vision, fostering a strong organizational culture that supports your growth objectives.

Assess Your Current Business Position

Evaluate your company's current position in relation to its mission and vision by conducting a comprehensive business analysis, as discussed in previous sections. This analysis should include an assessment of your financial performance, market share, competitive advantage, operational efficiency, customer satisfaction, employee engagement, and industry dynamics.

By understanding your business's current position, you can identify areas where you are excelling or falling short in fulfilling your mission and vision. This information provides a valuable foundation for setting growth goals that align with your company's core purpose and desired future state.

Set Growth Goals That Support Your Mission and Vision

With a clear understanding of your company's mission, vision, and current position, you can begin to set growth goals that align with these foundational principles. Your growth goals should be directly related to your mission and vision, supporting your business's core purpose and long-term aspirations.

For example, if your company's mission is to "improve people's lives through innovative healthcare solutions," a relevant growth goal might be to "expand our product offering to address unmet medical needs, reaching an additional 10% of the target market within the next three years."

Use the SMART Criteria for Setting Growth Goals

As mentioned in previous sections, using the SMART (Specific, Measurable, Achievable, Relevant, and Time-bound) criteria for setting growth goals ensures that they are well-defined, actionable, and trackable. Apply the SMART framework to your growth goals, ensuring that they align with your company's mission and vision.

Specific: Define your growth goal in clear and specific terms, outlining the desired outcome and the steps required to achieve it.

Measurable: Establish quantifiable metrics to track progress and measure success in relation to your mission and vision.

Achievable: Ensure that your growth goal is attainable, considering your business's current position, resources, and market conditions.

Relevant: Align your growth goal with your overall business mission and vision, ensuring that it supports your core purpose and long-term aspirations.

Time-bound: Set a deadline for achieving your growth goal, creating a sense of urgency and accountability.

Develop Strategies That Align with Your Mission and Vision

Once you have set growth goals that support your company's mission and vision, develop strategies and initiatives that align with these foundational principles. This may involve revisiting and refining your existing strategies or developing new ones to ensure they are consistent with your mission and vision.

For example, if your company's vision is to become "the most trusted provider of sustainable energy solutions," your growth strategies might involve investing in renewable energy technologies, partnering with environmentally conscious suppliers, or implementing energy-efficient practices across your operations.

Engage Your Team in the Alignment Process

Involving your team in the process of aligning growth goals with your company's mission and vision helps ensure that everyone understands and is committed to these objectives. Engage your team in setting growth goals, developing strategies, and implementing initiatives that support your mission and vision.

By fostering a shared understanding and commitment to your company's mission and vision, you create a strong organizational culture that supports your growth objectives and drives long-term success.

Communicate Your Aligned Growth Goals and Strategies

Transparently communicate your aligned growth goals and strategies to your team and stakeholders. Clearly explain how your growth objectives support your company's mission and vision, and outline the steps and resources required to achieve them.

Regular communication ensures that everyone within your organization remains focused on the growth goals and understands their role in achieving them. Moreover, transparent communication can help build trust and credibility with stakeholders, demonstrating your commitment to your company's mission and vision.

Monitor Progress and Adjust as Needed

Aligning growth goals with your company's mission and vision is an ongoing process that requires continuous monitoring and adjustment. Regularly review your progress against your growth goals and performance metrics to ensure that your strategies and initiatives are effectively supporting your mission and vision.

If you find that your growth goals are not being met or are diverging from your mission and vision, identify the underlying issues and adjust your strategies accordingly. Maintaining a strong alignment between your growth goals and your company's mission and vision ensures that your business remains focused on its core purpose and long-term aspirations, even as it grows and evolves.

Foster a Culture of Continuous Improvement

Cultivate a culture of continuous improvement within your organization by encouraging your team to regularly evaluate and refine your growth strategies and initiatives. By embracing a growth mindset and learning from both successes and challenges, your company can continuously adapt and improve, ensuring that your growth goals remain aligned with your mission and vision.

Balance Growth with Stability and Sustainability

As your business pursues its growth goals, it's crucial to maintain a balance between growth, stability, and sustainability. Rapid growth that compromises your company's financial stability, operational efficiency, or adherence to its mission and vision can undermine long-term success.

Regularly assess the impact of your growth strategies on your overall business health and adjust as needed to ensure that you maintain a strong alignment with your mission and vision while pursuing growth.

CHAPTER 2

MARKET ANALYSIS AND SEGMENTATION

Understanding and analyzing your target market is essential for identifying growth opportunities and developing effective strategies for business expansion. A comprehensive target market analysis can help you uncover unmet needs, emerging trends, and potential competitive advantages that can fuel your business growth. In this 3000-word guide, we will discuss the steps and methods for analyzing your target market to uncover growth opportunities.

Define Your Target Market

Before you can analyze your target market for growth opportunities, you need to clearly define who your target customers are. Consider the demographic, geographic, psychographic, and behavioral characteristics of the people most likely to benefit from your products or services. This information will help you create detailed customer personas, which can guide your market analysis and marketing strategies.

Conduct Market Research

Market research is the cornerstone of target market analysis, providing valuable insights into customer preferences, needs, and behaviors. There are two main types of market research: primary and secondary.

Primary Research: Primary research involves collecting data directly from your target customers through methods such as surveys, interviews, focus groups, and observations. This research can help you understand your customers' pain points, preferences, and purchasing habits, as well as identify potential growth opportunities.

Secondary Research: Secondary research involves analyzing existing data and information, such as industry reports, market studies, and competitor analyses. This research can provide insights into market size, trends, and competitive dynamics, helping you identify potential growth opportunities and challenges.

Analyze Market Size and Segmentation

Estimating the size and segmentation of your target market is crucial for identifying growth opportunities. Determine the total addressable market (TAM), which represents the maximum revenue potential for your product or service. Next, estimate the serviceable addressable market (SAM), which represents the portion of the TAM that you can realistically serve with your current business model, resources, and capabilities.

Divide your target market into segments based on shared characteristics, such as demographics, needs, or behaviors. This segmentation can help you identify underserved or high-potential market segments that present growth opportunities.

Identify and Analyze Market Trends

Understanding and anticipating market trends is essential for uncovering growth opportunities. Analyze industry reports, news articles, and expert opinions to identify emerging trends that could impact your target market, such as technological advancements, shifts in consumer preferences, or regulatory changes.

Consider how these trends could create new opportunities for your business, such as new product or service offerings, target market segments, or distribution channels. At the same time, be aware of potential challenges and risks associated with these trends and develop strategies to mitigate them.

Assess Customer Needs and Preferences

Gaining a deep understanding of your target customers' needs and preferences is crucial for identifying growth opportunities. Use your primary research findings, such as survey responses and interview transcripts, to uncover unmet needs, pain points, and desires among your target customers.

Consider how your business can address these needs and preferences through new or improved products or services, personalized marketing strategies, or enhanced customer experiences. By addressing unmet needs and preferences, you can create a competitive advantage and drive growth in your target market.

Evaluate Competitive Dynamics

Analyzing your competition is a critical component of target market analysis, as it can reveal both growth opportunities and potential challenges. Identify your main competitors and evaluate their strengths, weaknesses, opportunities, and threats (SWOT analysis).

Consider how your business can differentiate itself from competitors and capitalize on their weaknesses or gaps in their offerings. For example, you may be able to offer a superior product, more personalized service, or a more convenient delivery method. By understanding and exploiting competitive dynamics, you can position your business for growth in your target market.

Opportunities for Expansion

With a thorough understanding of your target

Identifying market niches and customer needs

Market, customer needs, market trends, and competitive dynamics, you can begin to explore opportunities for expansion. Consider the following growth strategies:

Market Penetration: Increase your market share within your existing target market by attracting new customers or encouraging existing customers to purchase more frequently or in larger quantities. This can be achieved through targeted marketing campaigns, promotional offers, or loyalty programs.

Market Development: Expand your business by entering new market segments or geographic regions. This could involve targeting a different demographic group, offering your products or services to a new industry, or expanding to new locations.

Product Development: Develop new or improved products or services to address unmet customer needs or take advantage of emerging market trends. This could involve enhancing existing offerings, creating complementary products, or developing entirely new solutions.

Diversification: Diversify your business by offering new products or services unrelated to your current offerings. This strategy can help reduce risk and increase revenue streams but requires careful planning and research to ensure success.

Develop and Implement Growth Strategies

Once you have identified growth opportunities in your target market, develop and implement strategies to capitalize on these opportunities. This may involve investing in product development, expanding your distribution channels, hiring additional staff, or launching new marketing campaigns.

Ensure that your growth strategies align with your overall business objectives, resources, and capabilities, and are supported by a detailed action plan outlining the steps, timelines, and resources required for successful execution.

Monitor and Evaluate Your Growth Strategies

As you implement your growth strategies, it's crucial to monitor their progress and evaluate their effectiveness in driving growth in your target market. Use performance metrics and key performance indicators (KPIs) to track the success of your strategies, such as customer acquisition cost, customer lifetime value, market share, or revenue growth.

Regularly review and adjust your growth strategies as needed, based on your performance data and any changes in market conditions or customer needs. This ongoing monitoring and evaluation process ensures that your growth strategies remain effective and relevant, maximizing your chances of success in your target market.

Foster a Growth-Oriented Organizational Culture

Creating and sustaining growth in your target market requires a growth-oriented organizational culture that encourages innovation, risk-taking, and continuous learning. Encourage your team to explore new ideas, challenge assumptions, and embrace change, and provide the resources and support necessary for them to succeed.

Recognize and reward your team's contributions to your business's growth, and ensure that they understand the link between their efforts and your target market growth objectives. By fostering a growth-oriented culture, you can empower your team to identify and capitalize on growth opportunities in your target market.

Crafting a unique value proposition to stand out

A unique value proposition (UVP) is a clear, concise statement that communicates the primary benefits of your product or service, differentiates your business from competitors, and compels your target audience to choose your offering over others. A strong UVP is crucial for attracting and retaining customers, as it positions your business as the best solution for their needs and preferences. In this 3000-word guide, we will discuss the steps and techniques for crafting a unique value proposition that helps your business stand out in a crowded market.

Understand Your Target Audience

Before crafting your UVP, it's essential to have a deep understanding of your target audience, including their needs, preferences, and pain points. Develop detailed customer personas that capture the demographic, geographic, psychographic, and behavioral characteristics of your ideal customers. Use these personas to guide your UVP development, ensuring that your messaging resonates with your target audience and addresses their specific needs and preferences.

Identify Your Key Differentiators

To craft a unique value proposition, you must first identify the key differentiators that set your product or service apart from competitors. These differentiators can include aspects such as product features, quality, pricing, customer service, or brand reputation. Consider conducting a competitive analysis to identify gaps in the market or areas where your business has a competitive advantage.

Focus on Customer Benefits

While it's essential to highlight your key differentiators, your UVP should ultimately focus on the benefits your product or service delivers to customers. These benefits can be functional (e.g., solving a problem or meeting a need), emotional (e.g., making customers feel good or relieving stress), or experiential (e.g., providing a unique user experience or exceptional customer service).

When crafting your UVP, consider how your key differentiators translate into tangible benefits for your customers. For example, if your product is made from high-quality materials, the benefit might be increased durability or enhanced performance.

Use Clear, Concise Language

A strong UVP should be easily understood and remembered by your target audience. Use clear, concise language that communicates your message quickly and effectively. Avoid jargon, buzzwords, or overly technical language that may confuse or alienate your audience. Instead, use simple, everyday language that your customers can relate to and understand.

Make It Specific and Measurable

To make your UVP more compelling and credible, include specific and measurable claims about the benefits your product or service delivers. For example, instead of saying "Our software saves you time," consider stating, "Our software reduces data entry time by 50%." Including specific, quantifiable information can help your audience better understand the value of your offering and make it more persuasive.

Test and Refine Your UVP

Once you have crafted your initial UVP, it's important to test it with your target audience to ensure it resonates with them and effectively communicates your unique value. This can involve conducting surveys, focus groups, or customer interviews to gather feedback on your UVP.

Use the feedback you receive to refine your UVP, addressing any areas of confusion, ambiguity, or lack of interest. Continue iterating on your UVP until you have a clear, compelling statement that effectively differentiates your business and appeals to your target audience.

Incorporate Your UVP into Your Branding and Marketing

Your unique value proposition should be a central element of your branding and marketing efforts. Incorporate your UVP into your brand messaging, marketing materials, website, and sales pitches to ensure a consistent and compelling message across all customer touchpoints.

By consistently communicating your UVP, you can build brand awareness and recognition, helping your business stand out in a crowded market and attract more customers.

Align Your UVP with Your Company's Mission and Vision

To ensure that your unique value proposition is authentic and sustainable, align it with your company's mission and vision. Your mission and vision should guide the development and execution of your UVP, as they represent your company's core purpose and long-term aspirations.

By aligning your UVP with your mission and vision, you can create a cohesive brand identity that resonates with your target audience and sets the foundation for long-term success.

Train Your Team on Your UVP

To ensure that your unique value proposition is effectively communicated and consistently delivered, train your team on your UVP and its importance to your business. Educate your team on the key differentiators and benefits that your UVP highlights, as well as the customer personas it is designed to appeal to.

By fostering a shared understanding of your UVP and its role in your business, you can empower your team to deliver exceptional customer experiences that reinforce your unique value proposition.

Continuously Review and Update Your UVP

As your business evolves and market conditions change, it's important to regularly review and update your unique value proposition to ensure it remains relevant and compelling. Conduct ongoing market research and customer feedback initiatives to stay informed of shifting customer needs, preferences, and competitive dynamics.

Use these insights to refine your UVP, ensuring that it continues to effectively differentiate your business and resonate with your target audience.

CHAPTER 3

DEVELOPING A SCALABLE BUSINESS MODEL

As your business grows, it's essential to evaluate the scalability of your current business model. Scalability refers to the ability of a business to expand and increase its capacity to meet rising demand, without compromising quality or customer satisfaction. In this 1000-word guide, we will discuss the factors to consider when evaluating your business model for scalability and how to address potential limitations.

Revenue Model

One of the first aspects to consider when evaluating your business model for scalability is your revenue model. Assess whether your current revenue streams can support growth without requiring significant additional resources or investments. Ideally, your revenue model should allow for incremental increases in revenue without proportional increases in costs.

Consider whether your current pricing structure, product mix, or sales channels can sustain growth. If not, you may need to explore alternative revenue models, such as subscription-based pricing, upselling or cross-selling, or entering new markets.

Cost Structure

Closely related to your revenue model is your cost structure. Evaluate whether your current costs are sustainable as your business scales. Consider both fixed costs (e.g., rent, salaries, equipment) and variable costs (e.g., materials, production, shipping) and identify potential areas for cost reduction or optimization.

Look for opportunities to leverage economies of scale, where costs per unit decrease as production volume increases, or implement cost-saving technologies, such as automation or process improvements. Ensuring a manageable cost structure is crucial for maintaining profitability as your business grows.

Operational Efficiency

Operational efficiency is a critical factor in determining the scalability of your business model. Analyze your current processes, systems, and workflows to identify bottlenecks, redundancies, or inefficiencies that could impede growth.

Consider whether your current technology infrastructure can support increased demand, or if upgrades or new systems are required. Streamlining operations and automating repetitive tasks can significantly improve efficiency and allow your business to scale more effectively.

Supply Chain Management

A robust and reliable supply chain is essential for scalable growth. Assess the capacity and flexibility of your current suppliers to accommodate increased demand. Consider whether you have sufficient backup suppliers in place to minimize disruptions and maintain production levels during periods of growth.

Evaluate your inventory management practices to ensure you can maintain adequate stock levels while minimizing carrying costs. As your business scales, consider implementing advanced inventory management systems or partnering with third-party logistics providers to optimize your supply chain.

Customer Service and Satisfaction

As your business grows, maintaining high levels of customer service and satisfaction is critical for retaining customers and attracting new ones. Evaluate whether your current customer service processes, staffing levels, and technology can support increased demand without compromising quality.

Consider implementing customer relationship management (CRM) systems or customer feedback tools to help manage customer interactions and track satisfaction levels. As your business scales, maintaining a strong focus on customer satisfaction can help ensure long-term success.

Human Resources and Talent Management

The scalability of your business model also depends on your ability to attract, retain, and develop the talent needed to support growth. Assess whether your current hiring, training, and retention practices can accommodate increased staffing needs.

Consider implementing talent management systems or partnering with external recruitment agencies to streamline your hiring process. As your business grows, ensuring that you have the right people in the right roles is crucial for maintaining operational efficiency and driving growth.

Market Demand and Competition

Finally, consider the market demand for your products or services and the competitive landscape in which your business operates. Evaluate whether there is sufficient market demand to support your growth ambitions, and assess your competitive position within your industry.

Identify potential barriers to entry or competitive threats that could limit your ability to scale, and develop strategies to address these challenges. Maintaining a strong competitive position and addressing market demand is essential for scalable growth Adaptability and Flexibility

Scalability also involves your business's ability to adapt and respond to changing market conditions, customer needs, or emerging opportunities. Assess your current business model's flexibility and adaptability, considering how quickly you can pivot or adjust your strategies to capitalize on new growth opportunities or address challenges.

Evaluate whether your organizational structure, decision-making processes, and company culture support adaptability and innovation. Cultivating a growth mindset and fostering a culture of continuous improvement can help your business remain agile and scalable in the face of change.

Financial Management and Access to Capital

Effective financial management and access to capital are crucial for supporting scalable growth. Evaluate your current financial management practices, including cash flow management, budgeting, and forecasting, to ensure they can accommodate increased demand and investment requirements.

Consider whether you have sufficient access to capital, either through internal resources or external financing options, to fund your growth initiatives. Establishing strong relationships with financial institutions, investors, or government funding programs can help secure the financial resources needed to scale your business.

Legal and Regulatory Compliance

As your business scales, it's essential to ensure that your operations remain compliant with all relevant legal and regulatory requirements. This includes industry-specific regulations, labor laws, taxation, and intellectual property protection.

Evaluate your current compliance practices and consider whether they can accommodate increased operational complexity or market expansion. Implementing robust compliance systems and seeking expert advice can help mitigate legal and regulatory risks as your business grows.

Adapting your operations to accommodate growth

As your business grows, it is crucial to adapt your operations to accommodate increased demand, maintain quality, and ensure customer satisfaction. In this 3000-word guide, we will discuss the steps and techniques for adapting your operations to support growth and long-term success.

Assess Your Current Operational Capacity

The first step in adapting your operations to accommodate growth is to assess your current operational capacity. This involves evaluating the capabilities and limitations of your existing infrastructure, processes, systems, and resources. Identify potential bottlenecks, inefficiencies, or resource constraints that could impede growth or negatively impact quality and customer satisfaction.

Develop a Growth Plan

Once you have assessed your current operational capacity, develop a comprehensive growth plan that outlines your business objectives, strategies, and actions required to achieve growth. This plan should consider all aspects of your operations, including production, supply chain, customer service, sales, marketing, and human resources.

Ensure that your growth plan is realistic and achievable, based on your current capacity and resources, and includes clear milestones, timelines, and performance indicators to track progress and measure success.

Optimize and Streamline Operations

As your business grows, it is essential to optimize and streamline your operations to improve efficiency, reduce costs, and maintain quality. This can involve implementing lean manufacturing principles, automating repetitive tasks, or redesigning workflows to eliminate redundancies and bottlenecks.

Consider investing in new technologies or systems that can help streamline operations, such as enterprise resource planning

(ERP) software, inventory management systems, or customer relationship management (CRM) tools.

Scale Production and Infrastructure

To accommodate growth, you may need to scale your production capacity and infrastructure to meet increased demand. This can involve expanding your existing facilities, investing in new equipment or technology, or outsourcing production to third-party manufacturers.

When scaling production, ensure that you maintain strict quality control processes to prevent any decline in product quality or customer satisfaction. Additionally, consider the environmental and social impacts of scaling production and implement sustainable practices to minimize any negative consequences.

Expand and Optimize Your Supply Chain

A robust and efficient supply chain is essential for supporting business growth. As your operations expand, assess the capacity and reliability of your current suppliers and consider whether you need to diversify or expand your supplier network to ensure a stable supply of materials and resources.

Optimize your inventory management practices to maintain adequate stock levels while minimizing carrying costs and reducing the risk of stockouts or obsolescence. Implement advanced inventory management systems or partner with third-party logistics providers to improve supply chain efficiency and support growth.

Enhance Customer Service and Support

As your customer base grows, it is crucial to maintain high levels of customer service and support to retain existing customers and attract new ones. Evaluate your current customer service processes and resources, and consider whether they can accommodate increased demand without compromising quality.

Invest in customer service training for your team, implement CRM systems to manage customer interactions, and consider offering new support channels, such as live chat or social media, to enhance customer satisfaction and loyalty.

Scale Your Sales and Marketing Efforts

To support business growth, you may need to scale your sales and marketing efforts to reach a larger audience and generate increased revenue. This can involve expanding your sales team, investing in new marketing channels or campaigns, or refining your sales and marketing strategies to target new customer segments or geographic regions.

Ensure that your sales and marketing efforts align with your growth objectives and are supported by a clear, compelling value proposition that differentiates your business and resonates with your target audience.

Invest in Human Resources and Talent Management

Supporting business growth requires investing in human resources and talent management to attract, retain, and develop the talent needed to drive growth. Evaluate your current hiring, training, and retention practices, and consider whether they can accommodate increased staffing needs or new skill requirements.

Implement talent management systems, such as applicant tracking software, to streamline your hiring process and improve candidate experience. Develop comprehensive onboarding and training programs to ensure new hires are well-equipped to succeed in their roles and contribute to your growth objectives.

Consider implementing performance management systems to track employee performance, identify high-potential talent, and facilitate career development. As your business grows, fostering a positive and supportive company culture is crucial for retaining top talent and maintaining high levels of employee engagement and satisfaction.

Maintain Effective Financial Management

As your operations expand to accommodate growth, effective financial management becomes even more critical. Ensure that your cash flow management, budgeting, and forecasting practices can support increased demand and investment requirements.

Monitor key financial performance indicators, such as profitability, revenue growth, and return on investment, to track your progress and inform decision-making. Implement financial management systems or work with external financial advisors to optimize your financial management practices and ensure the long-term financial stability of your growing business.

Ensure Legal and Regulatory Compliance

As your business grows and your operations become more complex, it's essential to ensure that you remain compliant with all relevant legal and regulatory requirements. This includes industry-specific regulations, labor laws, taxation, and intellectual property protection.

Evaluate your current compliance practices and consider whether they can accommodate increased operational complexity or market expansion. Implement robust compliance systems, seek expert legal advice, and conduct regular compliance audits to mitigate legal and regulatory risks as your business grows.

Foster a Culture of Continuous Improvement

Lastly, as your operations adapt to accommodate growth, it's crucial to foster a culture of continuous improvement and innovation within your organization. Encourage employees at all levels to identify and share ideas for improving processes, systems, products, or services.

Implement a formal continuous improvement program, such as the Plan-Do-Check-Act (PDCA) cycle or the Six Sigma methodology, to systematically identify, prioritize, and address areas for improvement. By cultivating a growth mindset and a culture of continuous improvement, you can ensure that your operations remain agile, efficient, and responsive to change as your business grows.

Leveraging technology to automate and streamline processes

As businesses grow and evolve, leveraging technology to automate and streamline processes becomes increasingly important to maintain efficiency, reduce costs, and enhance customer satisfaction. In this 3000-word guide, we will discuss the benefits of leveraging technology and explore various tools and strategies to automate and streamline processes across different areas of your business.

Benefits of Leveraging Technology

Leveraging technology offers numerous benefits for businesses, including:

Increased efficiency: Automation and streamlining can reduce manual labor, decrease processing times, and minimize errors, leading to significant improvements in operational efficiency.

Cost savings: By reducing the need for manual labor, technology can help lower labor costs and other operational expenses.

Enhanced customer satisfaction: Streamlined processes can lead to faster response times, more accurate order fulfillment, and improved overall customer experiences, ultimately contributing to higher levels of customer satisfaction and loyalty.

Scalability: Technology can enable businesses to scale their operations more effectively, accommodating increased demand without compromising quality or customer satisfaction.

Competitive advantage: Businesses that embrace technology can gain a competitive edge by offering superior products, services, or customer experiences, and by operating more efficiently than their competitors.

Identifying Processes for Automation and Streamlining

The first step in leveraging technology is to identify the processes within your business that could benefit from automation and streamlining. Some key areas to consider include:

Customer relationship management (CRM)

Sales and marketing

Order processing and fulfillment

Inventory management

Human resources and talent management

Financial management and accounting

Production and manufacturing

Analyze your current processes to pinpoint inefficiencies, bottlenecks, or areas that require significant manual labor. Consider conducting employee surveys or process audits to gather insights into potential areas for improvement.

Implementing Customer Relationship Management (CRM) Systems

CRM systems can help automate and streamline customer interactions and relationship management processes. These tools can centralize customer data, track interactions and sales activities, and generate reports and insights that enable more informed decision-making.

By implementing a CRM system, your business can automate repetitive tasks such as data entry and follow-up reminders, streamline the sales process, and enhance customer service by providing a more personalized and responsive experience.

Automating Sales and Marketing Processes

Technology can be used to automate various aspects of sales and marketing, including:

Email marketing: Use marketing automation tools to create, schedule, and track email campaigns, segment your audience, and personalize your messaging based on customer behavior.

Social media management: Use social media management tools to schedule and monitor social media posts, track engagement metrics, and analyze the performance of your social media campaigns.

Lead nurturing and scoring: Implement lead nurturing and scoring tools to automatically follow up with prospects, prioritize high-value leads, and identify those most likely to convert.

Sales process automation: Use sales automation tools to streamline tasks such as lead assignment, opportunity tracking, and sales forecasting.

Streamlining Order Processing and Fulfillment

Technology can help optimize order processing and fulfillment by:

- Integrating e-commerce platforms with inventory management systems to synchronize stock levels and streamline order processing.
- Automating order confirmation and shipping notifications to keep customers informed and reduce manual communication tasks.

- Implementing warehouse management systems to optimize inventory storage, picking, packing, and shipping processes.
- Utilizing shipping software to automate shipping label generation, carrier selection, and shipment tracking.

Optimizing Inventory Management

Automating and streamlining inventory management can help minimize stockouts, reduce carrying costs, and improve order fulfillment accuracy. Consider implementing:

- Inventory management software that tracks stock levels, automates reordering, and generates inventory reports.
- Barcode scanning and RFID technology to automate inventory tracking and reduce errors.
- Demand forecasting tools to analyze sales data and predict future inventory requirements, helping to optimize stock levels and reduce excess inventory.

Streamlining Human Resources and Talent Management

Technology can also help automate and streamline various aspects of human resources and talent management, including:

Recruiting and applicant tracking: Implement applicant tracking systems (ATS) to automate job postings, applicant screening, and interview scheduling, ultimately streamlining the recruitment process.

Onboarding and training: Utilize learning management systems (LMS) to automate employee onboarding and training, delivering consistent and accessible learning resources to new hires.

Performance management: Implement performance management software to automate goal setting, progress tracking, and performance reviews, helping to align employees with company objectives and foster career development.

Time and attendance tracking: Use time and attendance software to automate employee scheduling, time tracking, and leave management, minimizing manual labor and ensuring accurate payroll calculations.

Automating Financial Management and Accounting

Technology can be leveraged to automate and streamline various financial management and accounting processes, including:

Invoicing and billing: Implement invoicing software to automate invoice generation, payment tracking, and follow-up reminders, helping to improve cash flow management and reduce manual labor.

Expense management: Utilize expense management tools to streamline expense tracking, approval workflows, and reimbursement processes.

Payroll processing: Use payroll software to automate payroll calculations, tax filings, and direct deposit payments, ensuring accurate and timely payroll processing.

Financial reporting and analysis: Implement financial reporting and analytics tools to automate the generation of financial statements, budgets, and forecasts, providing real-time insights into your business's financial performance.

Optimizing Production and Manufacturing

For businesses involved in production or manufacturing, technology can be used to automate and streamline processes, such as:

Production planning and scheduling: Implement production planning software to optimize production schedules, balance workloads, and reduce lead times.

Manufacturing execution systems (MES): Use MES to monitor and control production processes, track work-in-progress, and analyze production data to identify areas for improvement.

Quality control and inspection: Utilize automated inspection systems, such as machine vision or sensor-based technologies, to ensure product quality and reduce manual inspection tasks.

Maintenance management: Implement computerized maintenance management systems (CMMS) to automate preventive maintenance scheduling, work order management, and asset tracking, ultimately extending the life of your equipment and minimizing downtime.

Measuring the Impact of Technology Implementation

After implementing technology to automate and streamline processes, it is crucial to measure the impact on your business's efficiency, cost savings, and customer satisfaction. Track relevant performance indicators, such as processing times, error rates, customer satisfaction scores, and return on investment (ROI) to evaluate the success of your technology initiatives and identify areas for further improvement.

CHAPTER 4

DIVERSIFYING YOUR REVENUE STREAMS

Expanding your product or service offerings is an essential aspect of business growth and sustainability. In this 3000-word guide, we will discuss the importance of diversifying your product or service portfolio and outline strategies to help you recognize and seize expansion opportunities.

The Importance of Expanding Product/Service Offerings

Expanding your product or service offerings can provide numerous benefits for your business, including:

Increased revenue streams: Diversifying your portfolio can generate additional revenue streams and reduce reliance on a single product or service.

Attracting new customers

Offering new products or services can help you tap into new market segments and attract a broader range of customers.

Retaining existing customers

Expanding your offerings can increase customer satisfaction and loyalty by providing a more comprehensive range of solutions that cater to different needs or preferences.

Enhancing your competitive advantage

A diversified product or service portfolio can differentiate your business from competitors and position you as a market leader.

Reducing risk

Relying on a single product or service can expose your business to market fluctuations or changing customer preferences. A diverse portfolio can help mitigate these risks and ensure business continuity.

Identifying Market Trends and Consumer Needs

To recognize opportunities for expanding your product or service offerings, it is crucial to stay informed about market trends and evolving consumer needs. Conduct regular market research to gather insights into industry trends, competitor activities, and customer preferences.

Consider utilizing various research methods, such as surveys, focus groups, interviews, or data analysis, to obtain a comprehensive understanding of the market landscape and identify potential opportunities for expansion.

Analyzing Your Existing Portfolio

Evaluate your current product or service offerings to identify strengths, weaknesses, and potential areas for improvement or expansion. Consider the following questions:

Which products or services are performing well, and why?

Are there any gaps in your current offerings that could be filled with new products or services?

Are there complementary products or services that could enhance the value of your existing offerings?

Conduct a SWOT analysis (Strengths, Weaknesses, Opportunities, and Threats) to assess your current portfolio and inform your expansion strategy.

Leveraging Your Core Competencies

One strategy for expanding your product or service offerings is to leverage your existing core competencies. These are the unique skills, knowledge, or resources that differentiate your business from competitors and provide a competitive advantage.

Consider how your core competencies could be applied to new product or service offerings. For example, a software development company with expertise in artificial intelligence could expand into new markets by developing AI-based solutions for different industries.

Exploring Adjacent Markets

Another approach to expanding your product or service offerings is to explore adjacent markets. These are markets that are closely related to your current market but offer new opportunities for growth. For example, a company that specializes in designing and manufacturing ergonomic office furniture could expand into the home office furniture market.

To identify adjacent markets, consider the following questions:

Which markets share similarities with your current market in terms of customer needs, preferences, or distribution channels?

Can your existing products or services be adapted to meet the needs of customers in adjacent markets?

Are there any emerging trends or technologies in adjacent markets that could present new opportunities for expansion?

Pursuing Strategic Partnerships or Acquisitions

Strategic partnerships or acquisitions can help you expand your product or service offerings by leveraging the expertise, resources, or market presence of another business. Consider partnering with or acquiring businesses that offer complementary products or services, have a strong market presence in your target segment, or possess valuable intellectual property or technology.

Ensure that any partnership or acquisition aligns with your overall business strategy and objectives, and conduct thorough due diligence to assess the potential risks and benefits.

7 Innovation is key to expanding your product or service offerings. Consider developing new products or services that cater to emerging customer needs or capitalize on market trends. When developing new offerings, keep the following considerations in mind:

Feasibility: Assess the technical, financial, and operational feasibility of developing and launching new products or services.

Market demand: Conduct market research to validate customer demand for your proposed offerings and identify potential market segments.

Competitive landscape: Analyze the competitive landscape to determine whether your new offerings can differentiate your business and provide a competitive advantage.

Time to market: Consider the time required to develop, test, and launch new products or services and assess the potential impact on your existing operations and resources.

Enhancing Your Existing Offerings

In some cases, expanding your product or service offerings may involve enhancing or updating your existing solutions. This can include:

- Adding new features or functionality to your products or services
- Improving product or service quality or performance
- Offering customized or personalized solutions
- Expanding your range of available product or service options
- Enhancing your existing offerings can help you maintain a competitive edge, increase customer satisfaction, and attract new customers.

Implementing a Go-to-Market Strategy

Once you have identified opportunities for expanding your product or service offerings, it is crucial to develop and implement a go-to-market strategy. This includes:

- Defining your target market segments and customer personas
- Developing a unique value proposition and messaging that clearly communicates the benefits of your new offerings
- Establishing pricing and distribution strategies
- Creating a marketing and sales plan to promote your new offerings and generate demand
- Allocating resources, such as personnel, budget, and technology, to support your expansion efforts

Monitor the performance of your new offerings and continuously iterate on your go-to-market strategy to optimize your results and achieve your growth objectives.

Evaluating the Impact of Product/Service Expansion

Regularly assess the impact of your product or service expansion efforts on your business's overall performance and growth. Track relevant performance indicators, such as revenue growth, market share, customer satisfaction, and return on investment (ROI) to evaluate the success of your expansion initiatives and identify areas for further improvement.

Exploring strategic partnerships and collaborations

In today's global economy, strategic partnerships and collaborations are becoming increasingly essential for businesses to stay competitive and grow. In this essay, we will explore the concept of strategic partnerships and collaborations, their benefits, and how they are formed. We will also examine the challenges of forming and managing such partnerships, and the strategies that businesses can use to overcome these challenges.

Definition of Strategic Partnerships and Collaborations:

Strategic partnerships and collaborations are formal agreements between two or more organizations to work together towards a common goal. These partnerships can take many forms, including joint ventures, licensing agreements, research and development partnerships, distribution agreements, and marketing collaborations.

Benefits of Strategic Partnerships and Collaborations:

There are several benefits of strategic partnerships and collaborations for businesses. These include:

Access to New Markets: By partnering with another business, a company can gain access to new markets that they may not have been able to enter otherwise.

Increased Resources: Partnerships can provide businesses with additional resources, including funding, expertise, and technology.

Reduced Costs: Collaborating with another business can help reduce costs by sharing resources and spreading out the costs of research and development.

Improved Innovation: By combining resources and expertise, businesses can create innovative products and services that they may not have been able to develop on their own.

Risk Mitigation: Partnerships can help businesses spread out risks by sharing them with their partners.

Forming Strategic Partnerships and Collaborations

There are several steps involved in forming strategic partnerships and collaborations:

1. **Identifying Potential Partners:** Businesses need to identify potential partners that can provide the resources and expertise they need.

2. **Establishing Objectives:** Once potential partners have been identified, businesses need to establish their objectives for the partnership, including what they hope to achieve and how they plan to do it.

3. **Negotiating the Partnership Agreement:** Businesses need to negotiate the terms of the partnership agreement, including the roles and responsibilities of each partner, the resources that each partner will provide, and how profits will be shared.

4. **Implementation:** Once the partnership agreement has been signed, the partners need to work together to implement the partnership, including developing new products and services and marketing them to customers.

Challenges of Strategic Partnerships and Collaborations

While there are many benefits of strategic partnerships and collaborations, there are also several challenges that businesses need to overcome in order to successfully form and manage these partnerships. These challenges include:

Cultural Differences: Businesses may have different cultures and ways of working, which can create communication and coordination challenges.

Power Imbalances: In some partnerships, one partner may have more power or resources than the other, which can create tension and conflict.

Conflicting Objectives: Partners may have conflicting objectives, which can make it difficult to reach agreement on key issues.

Legal Issues: Partnership agreements can be complex, and businesses may need to navigate legal issues such as intellectual property rights and non-disclosure agreements.

Strategies for Overcoming Challenges

There are several strategies that businesses can use to overcome the challenges of forming and managing strategic partnerships and collaborations:

Communication: Effective communication is key to successful partnerships. Businesses should establish clear lines of communication and regular meetings to ensure that everyone is on the same page.

Trust Building: Building trust between partners is essential for successful partnerships. This can be done through transparency, honesty, and consistent follow-through.

Flexibility: Partnerships require flexibility, as partners may need to adjust their objectives or plans as the partnership progresses.

Conflict Resolution: Businesses should establish processes for resolving conflicts, including mediation or arbitration.

Identifying new markets and customer segments

Identifying new markets and customer segments is a crucial aspect of business growth and development. It involves understanding the needs and preferences of potential customers in different regions and identifying opportunities to expand the business. In this section, we will discuss various strategies for identifying new markets and customer segments.

Conduct Market Research

Market research is the process of gathering information about potential customers, competitors, and market trends. It helps businesses to identify the needs and preferences of customers in different regions and to determine the demand for their products or services. This information can be collected through various methods, including surveys, focus groups, and online research.

Analyze Existing Customer Data

Analyzing existing customer data can help businesses to identify patterns and trends in customer behavior. It can also help them to understand the needs and preferences of their existing customers and to identify opportunities to expand their customer base. This data can be collected through customer surveys, customer feedback, and sales data.

Evaluate the Competition

Evaluating the competition is an important aspect of identifying new markets and customer segments. It involves researching competitors' products, services, and marketing strategies. This information can be used to identify gaps in the market and to develop a competitive advantage.

Explore New Distribution Channels

Exploring new distribution channels can help businesses to reach new customers and expand their market reach. This can involve partnering with other businesses, selling products or services online, or exploring new geographical regions.

Consider Cultural Differences

Cultural differences can play a significant role in customer preferences and behavior. Businesses should consider cultural differences when identifying new markets and customer segments. This can involve adapting products or services to suit local cultural preferences or marketing strategies that resonate with local customers.

Use Social Media

Social media is a powerful tool for identifying new markets and customer segments. It allows businesses to reach a global audience and to interact with potential customers in real-time. Social media platforms like Facebook, Twitter, and Instagram offer powerful targeting tools that can be used to reach specific customer segments.

Look for Emerging Trends

Identifying emerging trends can help businesses to stay ahead of the competition and to identify new opportunities for growth. This can involve monitoring industry publications, attending trade shows, and networking with other businesses.

Consider Geographic Expansion

Geographic expansion involves identifying new geographical regions to expand the business. This can involve partnering with local businesses or setting up new operations in the region. Businesses should consider factors such as language, culture, and infrastructure when identifying new markets for geographic expansion.

Identify Niche Markets

Identifying niche markets involves identifying specific customer segments with unique needs and preferences. These markets may be underserved by existing businesses and can offer significant opportunities for growth. Businesses should consider factors such as demographics, psychographics, and behavior when identifying niche markets.

Evaluate Customer Feedback

Customer feedback is an important source of information for identifying new markets and customer segments. It allows businesses to understand the needs and preferences of their customers and to identify opportunities for improvement. Businesses should actively solicit feedback from their customers and use it to guide their business decisions.

CHAPTER 5

BUILDING A STRONG BRAND IDENTITY

Building a strong brand identity is a key aspect of any successful business. It involves creating a unique and memorable identity that resonates with your target audience and sets your brand apart from competitors. One of the key components of a strong brand identity is crafting a compelling brand narrative. In this article, we will discuss the importance of a brand narrative and how to create one that resonates with your audience.

What is a Brand Narrative?

A brand narrative is the story that a brand tells about itself. It is a way of communicating the brand's values, mission, and unique identity to the world. A brand narrative is not just a list of facts or features, but a story that connects emotionally with the audience.

Why is a Brand Narrative Important?

A brand narrative is important because it helps to create a strong emotional connection between the brand and its audience. It humanizes the brand, making it relatable and memorable. A strong brand narrative can also help to differentiate a brand from its competitors, making it stand out in a crowded market.

How to Create a Compelling Brand Narrative?

Define Your Brand's Values and Mission

The first step in creating a compelling brand narrative is to define your brand's values and mission. What is your brand's purpose? What do you stand for? What are your core values? These are all questions that need to be answered before you can craft a meaningful brand narrative.

Identify Your Target Audience

The next step is to identify your target audience. Who are you trying to reach? What are their needs, wants, and desires? Understanding your target audience is critical to crafting a brand narrative that resonates with them.

Develop Your Brand Story

Once you have a clear understanding of your brand's values and mission and your target audience, it's time to develop your brand story. Your brand story should be authentic, engaging, and memorable. It should convey your brand's unique identity in a way that connects emotionally with your audience.

Use Emotion and Storytelling

Emotion and storytelling are critical components of a compelling brand narrative. People remember stories, not facts. Your brand narrative should tell a story that evokes emotion and connects with your audience on a deeper level. Use language and imagery that is evocative and memorable.

Be Consistent Across All Channels

Consistency is key when it comes to building a strong brand identity. Your brand narrative should be consistent across all channels, from your website and social media to your marketing materials and customer service. Consistency helps to reinforce your brand's identity and builds trust with your audience.

Incorporate Visual Elements

Visual elements such as logos, color schemes, and imagery are important components of a strong brand identity. Incorporate these elements into your brand narrative to create a cohesive and memorable brand identity.

Test and Refine Your Brand Narrative

Once you have developed your brand narrative, it's important to test and refine it over time. Solicit feedback from your audience and make adjustments as needed. A strong brand narrative is one that evolves and grows with your brand over time.

Consistently delivering on your brand promise

A brand promise is a commitment made by a company to its customers, and it represents what the company stands for and the experience customers can expect when they engage with the brand. It is an essential element of brand identity and plays a critical role in creating brand loyalty and building a strong reputation. Consistently delivering on your brand promise is essential for creating trust and loyalty with your customers, as well as for building a strong reputation and driving business success. In this article, we will discuss why delivering on your brand promise is important, and provide practical tips for doing so consistently.

Why Delivering on Your Brand Promise is Important?

Builds Trust and Loyalty with Customers

One of the most significant benefits of delivering on your brand promise is that it helps to build trust and loyalty with customers. When a company consistently delivers on its promises, it shows its customers that it is reliable, trustworthy, and committed to providing a positive experience. This, in turn, builds loyalty and encourages customers to return to the brand time and time again.

Enhances Brand Reputation

Delivering on your brand promise can also help to enhance your brand's reputation. When a company consistently delivers on its promises, it earns a reputation for being reliable, trustworthy, and committed to providing a positive experience. This can help to differentiate the brand from its competitors and create a positive image in the minds of customers.

Increases Customer Satisfaction

When a company delivers on its brand promise, it is more likely to meet the expectations of its customers. This, in turn, can lead to increased customer satisfaction, as customers feel that their needs are being met and their expectations are being exceeded. Satisfied customers are more likely to become repeat customers and to recommend the brand to others.

Drives Business Success

Finally, delivering on your brand promise can help to drive business success. When a company consistently delivers on its promises, it can increase customer loyalty, enhance its reputation, and improve customer satisfaction. This, in turn, can lead to increased sales, greater profitability, and a stronger competitive position in the market.

Tips for Consistently Delivering on Your Brand Promise

Define Your Brand Promise

The first step in consistently delivering on your brand promise is to define what that promise is. Your brand promise should be a clear, concise statement that represents what your brand stands for and the experience customers can expect when they engage with the brand. Once you have defined your brand promise, communicate it clearly to your employees and customers, so everyone understands what it means and what is expected.

Set Realistic Expectations

To consistently deliver on your brand promise, it is essential to set realistic expectations. Be honest with your customers about what they can expect from your brand, and do not promise more than you can deliver. Setting realistic expectations can help to prevent disappointment and ensure that customers have a positive experience.

Train Your Employees

Your employees play a critical role in delivering on your brand promise. They are the ones who interact with customers on a daily basis, and their actions and attitudes can have a significant impact on the customer experience. Providing training and support to your employees can help to ensure that they understand your brand promise and are equipped to deliver on it consistently.

Monitor and Measure Performance

Monitoring and measuring performance is essential for ensuring that you are delivering on your brand promise consistently. Regularly assess customer feedback, employee performance, and other metrics to identify areas for improvement and ensure that you are meeting your customers' expectations.

Communicate Regularly with Customers

Regular communication with customers can help to build trust and ensure that you are delivering on your brand promise consistently. This can involve soliciting feedback, providing updates on product or service developments, and responding promptly to customer inquiries and complaints. Communication can also help to identify areas for improvement and demonstrate your commitment to delivering a positive customer experience.

Continuously Improve Your Processes

To deliver on your brand promise consistently, it is essential to continuously improve your processes. Regularly assess your operations, identify areas for improvement, and implement changes as needed to ensure that you are delivering a positive customer experience.

Empower Your Employees

Empowering your employees can help to ensure that they are motivated and engaged in delivering on your brand promise. Provide them with the resources, training, and support they need to do their jobs effectively, and give them the autonomy to make decisions and solve problems on behalf of your customers.

Align Your Brand Promise with Your Business Strategy

Your brand promise should be aligned with your overall business strategy to ensure that you are delivering on your brand promise consistently. Make sure that your brand promise is reflected in your business operations, marketing messages, and customer interactions to create a seamless, unified experience for your customers.

Be Transparent and Accountable

Transparency and accountability are essential for delivering on your brand promise consistently. Be transparent with your customers about your policies, processes, and performance, and be accountable for your actions and decisions. When mistakes happen, take responsibility, and work to resolve them promptly to maintain trust and loyalty with your customers.

Stay Relevant and Responsive

Finally, staying relevant and responsive is essential for delivering on your brand promise consistently. Keep up with trends and changes in the market, and be responsive to your customers' needs and preferences. Continuously evolve and adapt your brand promise to ensure that it remains relevant and resonates with your target audience.

Using storytelling to connect with your audience

Storytelling is a powerful tool that businesses can use to connect with their audience. Stories have the ability to engage emotions, build connections, and inspire action. By incorporating storytelling into their marketing and communication strategies, businesses can create a more memorable and impactful experience for their audience. In this article, we will explore the benefits of storytelling and provide practical tips for using storytelling to connect with your audience.

The Benefits of Storytelling

There are some benefits of storytelling:

Engages Emotions

One of the primary benefits of storytelling is its ability to engage emotions. Stories have the power to evoke feelings of joy, sadness, excitement, and empathy, among others. When businesses use storytelling to connect with their audience, they can create a more emotional connection with their customers, which can help to build brand loyalty and trust.

Builds Connections

Storytelling can also help businesses to build connections with their audience. By sharing relatable stories and experiences, businesses can create a sense of community and shared values with their customers. This can help to build long-term relationships and create a loyal customer base.

Inspires Action

Another benefit of storytelling is its ability to inspire action. When businesses use storytelling to highlight the impact of their products or services, they can inspire their audience to take action and make a difference in their own lives or the lives of others. This can help to drive sales and create a positive impact in the world.

Tips for Using Storytelling to Connect with Your Audience

Know Your Audience

The first step in using storytelling to connect with your audience is to know who they are. Understanding your target audience's needs, values, and preferences can help you to create stories that resonate with them. Conduct market research, gather customer feedback, and analyze social media data to gain insights into your audience's behavior and preferences.

Identify Your Story

Once you understand your audience, the next step is to identify your story. Your story should be authentic, engaging, and relevant to your audience's interests and needs. Identify the key themes and values that define your brand, and use them to craft a compelling story that resonates with your audience.

Use Emotion

Emotion is a key element of storytelling. Use language and imagery that evokes emotion and connects with your audience on a deeper level. Show, don't tell, and use concrete examples and vivid descriptions to bring your story to life.

Keep it Simple

Simple stories are often the most effective. Avoid using technical jargon or overly complicated language that can confuse or alienate your audience. Use clear, concise language that is easy to understand and that communicates your message effectively.

Use Multiple Channels

Storytelling can be used across multiple channels, from social media to email marketing to video content. Consider the strengths and weaknesses of each channel and choose the ones that are most appropriate for your audience and message.

Be Consistent

Consistency is key when it comes to using storytelling to connect with your audience. Use a consistent brand voice, messaging, and imagery across all channels and touchpoints. This can help to reinforce your brand identity and build trust with your audience.

Highlight the Impact

Stories that highlight the impact of your products or services can be particularly powerful. Use real-world examples and customer testimonials to demonstrate the value of what you offer and the positive impact it can have on people's lives.

Be Authentic

Authenticity is essential for effective storytelling. Avoid using overly scripted or rehearsed stories that come across as insincere or inauthentic. Instead, use real stories and experiences that demonstrate your brand's values and mission.

Keep it Relevant

Finally, keep your storytelling relevant to your audience's interests and needs. Use stories that are timely and topical, and that address the issues and challenges that are important to your audience. This can help to capture their attention and create a more meaningful connection.

Examples of Effective Storytelling

Nike

Nike's "Just Do It" campaign is one of the most iconic examples of effective storytelling. The campaign focused on real-world athletes and their stories, demonstrating the dedication and passion required to achieve greatness. By highlighting the personal struggles and triumphs of real athletes, Nike was able to create a strong emotional connection with its audience and inspire them to pursue their own goals.

Airbnb

Airbnb's "Belong Anywhere" campaign is another example of effective storytelling. The campaign focused on the idea of travel as a way to connect with people and experience new cultures. By sharing stories of real travelers and their experiences, Airbnb was able to create a sense of community and shared values with its audience.

Patagonia

Patagonia is known for its commitment to sustainability and environmental stewardship, and its storytelling reflects this mission. The brand's "Worn Wear" campaign focused on the stories behind its products, highlighting the durability and longevity of its clothing and encouraging customers to repair and reuse their existing gear rather than buying new. By using storytelling to highlight the environmental impact of consumerism and the value of sustainability, Patagonia was able to create a deeper connection with its environmentally conscious audience.

CHAPTER 6

STRATEGIC MARKETING AND PROMOTION

A comprehensive marketing plan is an essential tool for businesses of all sizes and industries. A well-crafted marketing plan can help businesses to clarify their objectives, identify their target audience, develop effective messaging, and ultimately drive sales and revenue. In this article, we will discuss the key elements of a comprehensive marketing plan and provide practical tips for creating one that is tailored to your business's unique needs and goals.

Define Your Objectives

The first step in creating a comprehensive marketing plan is to define your objectives. What do you hope to achieve with your marketing efforts? Are you looking to increase brand awareness, generate leads, drive sales, or all of the above? Clarifying your objectives will help to guide your marketing strategy and ensure that you are focusing on the most important goals.

Identify Your Target Audience

The next step is to identify your target audience. Who are you trying to reach with your marketing efforts? What are their needs, wants, and preferences? Understanding your target audience is critical for developing messaging that resonates with them and creating a marketing strategy that effectively reaches and engages them.

Conduct a Competitive Analysis

Before developing your marketing strategy, it's important to conduct a competitive analysis. This involves researching your competitors to understand their strengths, weaknesses, and strategies. This information can help you to identify areas where you can differentiate your brand and develop a more effective marketing strategy.

Develop Your Messaging

Once you have a clear understanding of your objectives, target audience, and competitive landscape, it's time to develop your messaging. Your messaging should be tailored to your target audience and should communicate the value proposition of your products or services. It should be clear, concise, and memorable, and should differentiate your brand from competitors.

Choose Your Marketing Channels

There are a variety of marketing channels available, from social media and email marketing to paid advertising and content marketing. Choose the channels that are most appropriate for your business and target audience, and that align with your marketing objectives and budget.

Set Your Budget

Setting a marketing budget is an important step in creating a comprehensive marketing plan. Determine how much you are willing to spend on each marketing channel, and allocate your resources accordingly. Be sure to track your spending and adjust your strategy as needed based on the results.

Develop a Timeline

A timeline is essential for ensuring that your marketing efforts are executed on schedule and that you are able to achieve your objectives within your desired timeframe. Develop a timeline that includes specific deadlines for each aspect of your marketing plan, and be sure to monitor progress regularly.

Measure Your Results

Measuring the results of your marketing efforts is critical for evaluating the effectiveness of your strategy and making adjustments as needed. Use key performance indicators (KPIs) to track the success of your marketing campaigns and identify areas for improvement. Common KPIs include website traffic, conversion rates, social media engagement, and sales revenue.

Continuously Improve Your Strategy

Finally, it's important to continuously improve your marketing strategy based on your results and feedback from your target audience. Regularly review your marketing plan and make adjustments as needed to ensure that you are effectively reaching and engaging your audience and achieving your objectives.

Utilizing digital marketing channels for maximum reach

Digital marketing has become an essential component of modern business strategy. With the rise of the internet and social media, businesses now have more opportunities than ever before to reach their target audience and promote their products and services. In this article, we will discuss the key digital marketing channels that businesses can use to reach their audience and provide tips for maximizing their reach.

Search Engine Optimization (SEO)

Search Engine Optimization (SEO) involves optimizing your website and online content to improve its ranking in search engine results pages. By improving your ranking, you can increase your visibility and reach a wider audience. Some tips for maximizing your SEO include:

- Conducting keyword research to identify the search terms your target audience is using
- Creating high-quality, relevant content that incorporates those keywords
- Ensuring that your website is mobile-friendly and easy to navigate

- Building high-quality backlinks to your website from other reputable sites

Pay-Per-Click (PPC) Advertising

Pay-Per-Click (PPC) advertising involves placing ads on search engine results pages and other websites and paying a fee each time a user clicks on your ad. PPC advertising can be a highly effective way to reach your target audience and drive traffic to your website. Some tips for maximizing your PPC advertising include:

- Conducting keyword research to identify the search terms your target audience is using
- Creating compelling ad copy and calls to action
- Targeting your ads to specific demographics, locations, and interests
- Continuously monitoring and optimizing your campaigns based on performance data

Social Media Marketing

Social media marketing involves using social media platforms like Facebook, Twitter, and Instagram to promote your brand and engage with your audience. Social media can be a powerful tool for building brand awareness, driving engagement, and generating leads. Some tips for maximizing your social media marketing include:

- Creating a consistent brand voice and messaging across all social media channels
- Identifying the social media platforms that are most relevant to your target audience
- Developing a content calendar and regularly posting high-quality content that resonates with your audience
- Using social media analytics to track performance and adjust your strategy as needed

Content Marketing

Content marketing involves creating and distributing valuable, relevant content to attract and engage your target audience. Content marketing can help to build brand awareness, establish thought leadership, and drive traffic to your website. Some tips for maximizing your content marketing include:

- Conducting keyword research to identify the search terms your target audience is using
- Creating high-quality, relevant content that incorporates those keywords
- Using a variety of content formats, including blog posts, infographics, videos, and podcasts
- Promoting your content through social media, email marketing, and other channels

Email Marketing

Email marketing involves sending targeted, personalized emails to your audience to promote your products and services. Email marketing can be a highly effective way to build relationships with your audience and drive sales. Some tips for maximizing your email marketing include:

- Segmenting your email list based on demographics, interests, and behaviors
- Personalizing your emails with the recipient's name and other relevant information
- Creating compelling subject lines and calls to action
- Regularly testing and optimizing your email campaigns based on performance data

Influencer Marketing

Influencer marketing involves partnering with influencers in your industry or niche to promote your brand and products. Influencer marketing can be a highly effective way to reach new audiences and build trust with your target audience. Some tips for maximizing your influencer marketing include:

- Identifying influencers who align with your brand values and target audience
- Developing a clear partnership agreement that outlines expectations and compensation

- Providing influencers with high-quality products or services to promote
- Regularly monitoring and measuring the performance of your influencer marketing campaigns

Implementing targeted advertising campaigns

Targeted advertising campaigns are a highly effective way to reach your desired audience and drive conversions. By using data and insights to tailor your ads to specific demographics, interests, and behaviors, you can increase the relevance and effectiveness of your campaigns. In this article, we will discuss the key steps involved in implementing targeted advertising campaigns and provide tips for maximizing their impact.

Define Your Target Audience

The first step in implementing a targeted advertising campaign is to define your target audience. This involves identifying the demographics, interests, and behaviors of the people you want to reach with your ads. Some key factors to consider when defining your target audience include:

- Age
- Gender
- Geographic location
- Education level
- Income level

- Interests and hobbies
- Buying habits

By understanding your target audience, you can create ads that resonate with their interests and needs and increase the likelihood of conversion.

Choose Your Advertising Channels

Once you have defined your target audience, the next step is to choose the advertising channels that are most appropriate for reaching them. There are a variety of advertising channels available, including:

1. Search engine advertising (such as Google Ads)
2. Social media advertising (such as Facebook Ads)
3. Display advertising (such as banner ads)
4. Video advertising (such as YouTube Ads)

Consider the strengths and weaknesses of each channel and choose the ones that are most appropriate for your target audience and advertising goals.

Develop Your Creative

Once you have chosen your advertising channels, the next step is to develop your creative. Your creative should be tailored to your target audience and should be designed to capture their attention and encourage them to take action. Some tips for developing effective creative include:

1. Using high-quality visuals and graphics
2. Incorporating compelling headlines and calls to action
3. Tailoring your messaging to your target audience's interests and needs
4. Using A/B testing to optimize your creative for maximum effectiveness

Set Your Budget

Setting a budget is an important step in implementing a targeted advertising campaign. Determine how much you are willing to spend on each advertising channel and allocate your resources accordingly. Be sure to track your spending and adjust your strategy as needed based on the results.

Set Your Targeting Parameters

Setting your targeting parameters involves using data and insights to tailor your ads to specific demographics, interests, and behaviors. Some common targeting parameters include:

1. Age and gender
2. Geographic location
3. Education level and income level
4. Interests and hobbies
5. Buying habits and purchasing history

By setting your targeting parameters, you can ensure that your ads are reaching the right people and increasing the likelihood of conversion.

Monitor and Optimize Your Campaigns

Monitoring and optimizing your campaigns is essential for maximizing their impact. Regularly review your campaign performance data and adjust your strategy as needed based on the results. Some key performance indicators (KPIs) to track include:

- Click-through rates (CTR)
- Conversion rates
- Return on investment (ROI)
- Cost per acquisition (CPA)

By regularly monitoring and optimizing your campaigns, you can ensure that you are reaching your target audience and achieving your advertising goals.

Leverage Retargeting

Retargeting involves using data to target ads to people who have already interacted with your brand or visited your website. By targeting these people with ads that are tailored to their interests and needs, you can increase the likelihood of conversion and drive sales. Some tips for leveraging retargeting include:

1. Using data to segment your retargeting audience based on behavior and interests
2. Developing tailored messaging and creative that addresses the specific needs and interests of your retargeting audience
3. Setting frequency caps to avoid over-exposure and fatigue
4. Regularly monitoring and optimizing your retargeting campaigns based on performance data

CHAPTER 7

CUSTOMER RETENTION AND LOYALTY

In today's highly competitive business environment, delivering exceptional customer experiences has become essential for building brand loyalty, driving sales, and achieving long-term success. A positive customer experience can create a lasting impression, encourage repeat business, and generate positive word-of-mouth referrals. In this article, we will discuss the key elements of delivering exceptional customer experiences and provide tips for maximizing their impact.

Understand Your Customers

The first step in delivering exceptional customer experiences is to understand your customers. This involves identifying their needs, preferences, and pain points, and tailoring your products, services, and interactions to meet those needs. Some key factors to consider when understanding your customers include:

1. Demographics (age, gender, location, etc.)
2. Buying habits and purchasing history
3. Interests and preferences
4. Pain points and challenges

By understanding your customers, you can create products, services, and interactions that are tailored to their needs and increase the likelihood of customer satisfaction and loyalty.

Create a Positive First Impression

Creating a positive first impression is essential for delivering exceptional customer experiences. The first few seconds of an interaction can set the tone for the entire experience, so it's important to make a positive impression from the start. Some tips for creating a positive first impression include:

1. Greeting customers warmly and with enthusiasm
2. Being attentive and listening actively
3. Being knowledgeable about your products and services
4. Providing clear and concise information

By creating a positive first impression, you can establish a foundation of trust and rapport that can lead to a positive overall experience.

Be Responsive and Empathetic

Being responsive and empathetic is essential for delivering exceptional customer experiences. When customers reach out with questions, concerns, or issues, it's important to respond in a timely manner and to demonstrate empathy for their situation. Some tips for being responsive and empathetic include:

- Responding to customer inquiries promptly and with personalized messages
- Listening actively and acknowledging the customer's concerns
- Apologizing when appropriate and taking responsibility for mistakes
- Offering solutions and options to resolve issues

By being responsive and empathetic, you can demonstrate that you value your customers and their experiences, and increase the likelihood of customer satisfaction and loyalty.

Provide Consistent and Reliable Service

Providing consistent and reliable service is essential for delivering exceptional customer experiences. Customers expect a consistent level of quality and service, and it's important to meet those expectations consistently over time. Some tips for providing consistent and reliable service include:

- Setting clear expectations for service quality and delivery
- Training employees to deliver consistent and reliable service
- Monitoring performance and service quality regularly
- Soliciting feedback from customers and using it to improve service quality

By providing consistent and reliable service, you can establish a reputation for quality and dependability, and increase the likelihood of customer satisfaction and loyalty.

Personalize the Experience

Personalizing the customer experience is essential for delivering exceptional customer experiences. Customers expect a personalized experience that is tailored to their needs, preferences, and interests. Some tips for personalizing the experience include:

1. Using customer data and insights to tailor products and services to customer needs
2. Providing personalized recommendations and offers based on customer preferences and behavior
3. Addressing customers by name and using personalized messages
4. Providing personalized follow-up and support after the sale

By personalizing the experience, you can demonstrate that you value your customers as individuals and increase the likelihood of customer satisfaction and loyalty.

Use Technology to Enhance the Experience

Using technology to enhance the customer experience can be a highly effective way to deliver exceptional customer experiences. Technology can streamline processes, personalize interactions, and create a seamless experience across channels. Some tips for using technology to enhance the experience include:

- Providing self-service options that allow customers to access information and complete transactions on their own
- Offering personalized recommendations and offers based on customer data and insights
- Using chatbots and other artificial intelligence tools to provide quick and personalized customer service
- Creating a seamless experience across channels, such as website, social media, and mobile apps

By using technology to enhance the experience, you can create a more efficient, personalized, and engaging experience for your customers.

Empower Employees to Deliver Exceptional Service

Empowering employees to deliver exceptional service is essential for delivering exceptional customer experiences. Employees are often the frontline of customer interactions and it's important to provide them with the training, tools, and autonomy they need to deliver high-quality service. Some tips for empowering employees include:

- Providing comprehensive training on product knowledge, customer service, and communication skills
- Encouraging employees to take ownership of customer interactions and to solve problems creatively
- Empowering employees to make decisions and to offer personalized solutions to customers
- Recognizing and rewarding employees who deliver exceptional service

By empowering employees to deliver exceptional service, you can create a culture of service excellence and increase the likelihood of customer satisfaction and loyalty.

Measure and Optimize the Customer Experience

Measuring and optimizing the customer experience is essential for delivering exceptional customer experiences. By tracking customer satisfaction, feedback, and behavior, you can identify areas for improvement and optimize your service delivery accordingly. Some tips for measuring and optimizing the customer experience include:

- Collecting customer feedback through surveys, reviews, and social media channels
- Using customer data and analytics to track behavior and preferences
- Using A/B testing to optimize service delivery and messaging

- Continuously monitoring and adjusting your service delivery based on customer feedback and behavior

By measuring and optimizing the customer experience, you can identify areas for improvement and continually enhance the experience for your customers.

Implementing customer loyalty programs

Customer loyalty programs are a highly effective way to incentivize repeat business, build brand loyalty, and increase customer lifetime value. By offering rewards, discounts, and other incentives to loyal customers, businesses can create a sense of loyalty and foster a deeper connection with their customer base. In this article, we will discuss the key elements of implementing customer loyalty programs and provide tips for maximizing their impact.

Define Your Objectives

The first step in implementing a customer loyalty program is to define your objectives. What do you hope to achieve through your loyalty program? Some common objectives include:

o Increasing customer retention and repeat business
o Encouraging customer referrals and word-of-mouth marketing
o Collecting customer data and insights for marketing purposes

o   Increasing customer lifetime value

By defining your objectives, you can create a loyalty program that is tailored to your business goals and will be most effective in achieving those goals.

Choose Your Rewards

Choosing your rewards is a key element of implementing a customer loyalty program. Rewards can include discounts, free products or services, exclusive offers, and more. Some tips for choosing your rewards include:

1. Offering rewards that are relevant and valuable to your target audience
2. Varying your rewards to keep customers engaged and interested
3. Offering rewards that align with your brand values and messaging
4. Setting achievable reward levels that encourage customer participation

By choosing the right rewards, you can incentivize customer participation and build loyalty.

Design Your Program Structure

Designing your program structure is another key element of implementing a customer loyalty program. Your program structure should be clear, easy to understand, and easy to participate in. Some tips for designing your program structure include:

- o Setting clear guidelines for participation, rewards, and redemption
- o Making it easy for customers to enroll and participate in the program
- o Offering multiple ways for customers to earn and redeem rewards
- o Creating a tiered structure that rewards customers for increasing levels of participation

By designing a clear and easy-to-understand program structure, you can encourage participation and build loyalty.

Promote Your Program

Promoting your program is essential for building awareness and encouraging participation. Some tips for promoting your program include:

- o Creating a dedicated landing page on your website for the loyalty program
- o Promoting your program through email marketing, social media, and other channels
- o Offering a sign-up bonus to encourage participation
- o Creating promotional materials, such as flyers, brochures, and posters, to promote the program

By promoting your program effectively, you can build awareness and encourage participation.

Track and Analyze Program Performance

Tracking and analyzing program performance is essential for optimizing your program and maximizing its impact. Some key metrics to track include:

- o Participation rates
- o Redemption rates
- o Customer retention rates
- o Customer lifetime value
- o Referral rates

By tracking and analyzing program performance, you can identify areas for improvement and optimize your program accordingly.

Continuously Optimize Your Program

Continuously optimizing your program is essential for maximizing its impact over time. Some tips for optimizing your program include:

- o Soliciting feedback from customers and incorporating it into program design and implementation
- o Offering new and varied rewards to keep customers engaged and interested

- Testing and refining program structure and rewards based on performance data
- Continuously monitoring and analyzing program performance to identify areas for improvement
- By continuously optimizing your program, you can ensure that it remains effective and impactful over time.

Use Customer Data and Insights to Personalize the Experience

Using customer data and insights to personalize the experience is essential for creating a deeper connection with your customers and building loyalty. Some tips for using customer data and insights include:

- Collecting customer data and insights through loyalty program participation and other interactions
- Using customer data and insights to tailor rewards and offers to individual customer preferences
- Personalizing program messaging and communications based on customer data and preferences
- Using data and insights to segment customers and create targeted promotions and offers
- Analyzing customer data and behavior to identify opportunities for personalization and customization

By using customer data and insights to personalize the experience, you can create a deeper connection with your customers and increase the likelihood of loyalty.

Make the Program Easy to Use and Redeem

Making the program easy to use and redeem is essential for maximizing its impact. Customers should be able to participate in the program and redeem rewards with minimal effort and hassle. Some tips for making the program easy to use and redeem include:

a. Offering multiple ways for customers to participate in the program, such as through a mobile app or website

b. Streamlining the redemption process to minimize hassle and wait times

c. Making it easy for customers to track their rewards and progress

d. Offering customer support and assistance for program participation and redemption

By making the program easy to use and redeem, you can encourage participation and build loyalty.

Align the Program with Your Brand Values and Messaging

Aligning the program with your brand values and messaging is essential for creating a cohesive and effective loyalty program. The program should reflect your brand identity and values and be consistent with your messaging across channels. Some tips for aligning the program with your brand values and messaging include:

a. Ensuring that rewards and offers align with your brand identity and values

b. Creating program messaging that reflects your brand voice and tone

c. Incorporating your brand visuals and design into program materials and communications

d. Ensuring that the program is consistent with your messaging across channels

By aligning the program with your brand values and messaging, you can create a more cohesive and effective program.

Encouraging customer feedback and continuously improving

Encouraging customer feedback and continuously improving is essential for businesses that want to remain competitive and relevant in today's rapidly changing marketplace. By soliciting feedback from customers and using that feedback to make meaningful improvements to products, services, and customer experiences, businesses can stay ahead of the curve and maintain a competitive edge. In this article, we will discuss the key elements of encouraging customer feedback and continuously improving, and provide tips for maximizing their impact.

Create a Culture of Feedback

The first step in encouraging customer feedback and continuously improving is to create a culture of feedback within your organization. This involves instilling a mindset of continuous improvement and encouraging all employees to actively seek out and welcome feedback from customers. Some tips for creating a culture of feedback include:

o   Providing training on how to solicit and receive feedback

o   Creating a safe and open environment for feedback, where customers feel comfortable sharing their opinions and concerns

o   Rewarding employees who solicit and incorporate customer feedback into their work

o   Using customer feedback as a basis for decision-making across the organization

By creating a culture of feedback, you can establish a foundation for continuous improvement and encourage employees to take ownership of customer experiences.

Solicit Feedback Proactively

Soliciting feedback proactively is essential for encouraging customer feedback and continuously improving. Rather than waiting for customers to offer feedback, businesses should actively seek it out through surveys, social media, focus groups, and other channels. Some tips for soliciting feedback proactively include:

- o Offering incentives for feedback, such as discounts or free products
- o Using multiple channels to solicit feedback, including email, social media, and mobile apps
- o Asking specific questions that are relevant to customer experiences and pain points
- o Using feedback to inform future product development and service improvements

By soliciting feedback proactively, you can gain valuable insights into customer experiences and identify areas for improvement.

Respond to Feedback Promptly and Thoughtfully

Responding to feedback promptly and thoughtfully is essential for building trust and encouraging further feedback. When customers take the time to provide feedback, it's important to acknowledge their input and respond in a timely manner. Some tips for responding to feedback promptly and thoughtfully include:

- o Acknowledging the feedback and thanking the customer for their input
- o Addressing the specific concerns or issues raised in the feedback

o   Offering solutions or remedies to address the concerns

o   Following up with the customer to ensure that their concerns have been addressed

By responding to feedback promptly and thoughtfully, you can build trust and encourage further feedback from customers.

Analyze Feedback and Identify Themes

Analyzing feedback and identifying themes is essential for making meaningful improvements based on customer input. By aggregating feedback and identifying recurring themes, businesses can identify areas for improvement and make data-driven decisions. Some tips for analyzing feedback and identifying themes include:

- Using software tools to aggregate and analyze feedback
- Categorizing feedback into common themes, such as product quality or customer service
- Identifying trends and patterns in feedback over time
- Prioritizing areas for improvement based on the frequency and severity of customer concerns

By analyzing feedback and identifying themes, businesses can make targeted improvements that have the greatest impact on customer satisfaction.

Make Improvements Based on Feedback

Making improvements based on feedback is essential for continuously improving and staying ahead of the curve. Businesses should use customer feedback to inform product development, service improvements, and customer experience enhancements. Some tips for making improvements based on feedback include:

> ➢ Prioritizing improvements based on the severity and frequency of customer concerns
> ➢ Testing improvements before implementing them across the organization
> ➢ Communicating changes to customers and seeking feedback on the effectiveness of the improvements
> ➢ Continuously monitoring and analyzing the impact of improvements on customer satisfaction

By making improvements based on feedback, businesses can create a culture of continuous improvement.

Share the Results of Customer Feedback

Sharing the results of customer feedback is essential for maintaining transparency and building trust with customers. By sharing feedback and the resulting improvements, businesses can show customers that their opinions are valued and that the business is committed to making meaningful improvements. Some tips for sharing the results of customer feedback include:

- ❖ Creating a feedback summary report that highlights key feedback themes and the resulting improvements
- ❖ Sharing the report with all employees and making it available to customers
- ❖ Highlighting specific customer feedback that led to significant improvements
- ❖ Communicating the results of customer feedback through multiple channels, such as email, social media, and website updates

By sharing the results of customer feedback, businesses can build trust and credibility with their customer base.

Continuously Monitor and Analyze Feedback

Continuously monitoring and analyzing feedback is essential for maintaining a culture of continuous improvement. Businesses should regularly collect and analyze feedback to identify new opportunities for improvement and to ensure that existing improvements are effective. Some tips for continuously monitoring and analyzing feedback include:

a. Setting up a regular feedback collection schedule, such as quarterly or bi-annually
b. Analyzing feedback data to identify trends and patterns over time
c. Monitoring social media channels and review sites for customer feedback

d. Using software tools to track and analyze feedback across multiple channels

By continuously monitoring and analyzing feedback, businesses can stay ahead of changing customer needs and expectations.

Use Feedback to Differentiate Your Business

Using feedback to differentiate your business is a highly effective way to stand out in a crowded marketplace. By incorporating customer feedback into your marketing messaging and branding, businesses can demonstrate their commitment to customer satisfaction and differentiate themselves from competitors. Some tips for using feedback to differentiate your business include:

a. Incorporating customer testimonials and feedback into marketing materials
b. Highlighting customer satisfaction ratings and improvements in branding
c. Communicating the results of customer feedback in press releases and other media
d. Creating customer feedback-driven awards or recognition programs

By using feedback to differentiate your business, you can set yourself apart from competitors and establish yourself as a leader in customer satisfaction.

Encouraging customer feedback and continuously improving is essential for businesses that want to remain competitive and relevant in today's rapidly changing marketplace. By creating a culture of feedback, soliciting feedback proactively, responding to feedback promptly and thoughtfully, analyzing feedback and identifying themes, making improvements based on feedback, sharing the results of customer feedback, continuously monitoring and analyzing feedback, and using feedback to differentiate your business, businesses can establish a customer-centric culture that drives long-term success.

CHAPTER 8

BUILDING A HIGH-PERFORMANCE TEAM

Building a high-performance team is essential for businesses that want to achieve long-term success. A high-performance team is one that is able to consistently exceed expectations and deliver exceptional results. In this article, we will discuss the key elements of building a high-performance team, with a focus on hiring and retaining top talent.

Define Your Needs

The first step in building a high-performance team is to define your needs. This involves identifying the skills, experience, and attributes that are essential for success in the role. Some tips for defining your needs include:

- ❖ Identifying the core competencies required for success in the role
- ❖ Creating a job description that accurately reflects the skills, experience, and attributes required
- ❖ Identifying any gaps in your existing team and identifying candidates who can fill those gaps
- ❖ Developing a comprehensive recruitment plan that targets the right candidates

By defining your needs, you can ensure that you are targeting the right candidates and setting yourself up for success.

Develop a Strong Employer Brand

Developing a strong employer brand is essential for attracting top talent. An employer brand is the perception that potential employees have of your organization as a place to work. Some tips for developing a strong employer brand include:

Building a positive company culture that values employee satisfaction and engagement

- ➤ Offering competitive compensation and benefits packages
- ➤ Providing opportunities for career advancement and professional development
- ➤ Establishing a clear mission, vision, and values that align with your employees' goals and values

By developing a strong employer brand, you can attract top talent and set yourself apart from competitors.

Utilize Multiple Recruitment Channels

Utilizing multiple recruitment channels is essential for reaching a diverse pool of candidates. Some tips for utilizing multiple recruitment channels include:

1. Posting job openings on job boards and professional networking sites
2. Partnering with recruitment agencies or headhunters
3. Utilizing social media channels to reach potential candidates
4. Networking at industry events and conferences

By utilizing multiple recruitment channels, you can reach a diverse pool of candidates and increase your chances of finding the right fit for your team.

Conduct Rigorous Interviews

Conducting rigorous interviews is essential for identifying the best candidates for your team. Some tips for conducting rigorous interviews include:

➤ Asking behavioral questions that assess the candidate's past performance and how they approach problem-solving

➤ Using assessment tools to evaluate the candidate's skills and fit for the role

➤ Conducting multiple rounds of interviews to gain a deeper understanding of the candidate's skills, experience, and personality

➤ Involving other members of the team in the interview process to gain different perspectives

By conducting rigorous interviews, you can ensure that you are identifying the best candidates for your team.

Offer Competitive Compensation and Benefits

Offering competitive compensation and benefits is essential for attracting and retaining top talent. Some tips for offering competitive compensation and benefits include:

> ➤ Researching industry standards to ensure that your compensation and benefits packages are competitive
> ➤ Offering additional perks and benefits, such as flexible work arrangements and employee wellness programs
> ➤ Providing opportunities for bonuses and incentives based on performance and company success

By offering competitive compensation and benefits, you can attract and retain top talent and motivate your team to perform at their best.

Foster a Positive Company Culture

Fostering a positive company culture is essential for building a high-performance team. A positive company culture is one that values collaboration, open communication, and employee satisfaction. Some tips for fostering a positive company culture include:

> ➤ Encouraging open communication and collaboration among team members

- Offering opportunities for team-building and social events
- Providing regular feedback and recognition for good performance
- Encouraging employee development and professional growth
- By fostering a positive company culture, you can build a team that is motivated and engaged in their work.

Offer Opportunities for Professional Development

Offering opportunities for professional development is essential for retaining top talent and ensuring that your team is equipped to perform at their best. Some tips for offering opportunities for professional development include:

- Offering training and development programs that are relevant to the skills and experience required for the role
- Providing opportunities for employees to attend industry events and conferences
- Encouraging employees to pursue additional certifications or degrees
- Providing mentoring and coaching programs to help employees develop their skills and advance their careers

By offering opportunities for professional development, you can retain top talent and ensure that your team is equipped with the skills and knowledge needed to perform at their best.

Provide Regular Feedback and Performance Evaluations

Providing regular feedback and performance evaluations is essential for helping employees understand how they can improve and grow within the organization. Some tips for providing regular feedback and performance evaluations include:

1. Setting clear performance expectations and goals
2. Providing regular feedback on progress towards goals
3. Conducting regular performance evaluations to assess employee performance and identify areas for improvement
4. Offering coaching and development opportunities based on performance evaluations

By providing regular feedback and performance evaluations, you can help employees understand their strengths and areas for improvement and support their growth within the organization.

Build Strong Relationships with Your Team

Building strong relationships with your team is essential for creating a positive and productive work environment. Some tips for building strong relationships with your team include:

➢ Communicating openly and transparently with your team
➢ Encouraging feedback and ideas from team members
➢ Showing appreciation and recognition for good work

➤ Providing opportunities for team-building and social events

By building strong relationships with your team, you can create a culture of trust and collaboration that supports high performance.

Cultivating a growth-oriented company culture

Cultivating a growth-oriented company culture is essential for businesses that want to achieve long-term success. A growth-oriented culture is one that values innovation, creativity, and continuous improvement. In this article, we will discuss the key elements of cultivating a growth-oriented company culture.

Establish a Clear Mission, Vision, and Values

Establishing a clear mission, vision, and values is essential for creating a growth-oriented company culture. A clear mission, vision, and values statement provides a shared sense of purpose and direction for the organization, and helps employees understand how their work contributes to the overall goals of the company. Some tips for establishing a clear mission, vision, and values include:

Involving employees in the development of the mission, vision, and values statement

Communicating the statement regularly and consistently to all employees

Ensuring that the statement is aligned with the goals and objectives of the organization

Incorporating the statement into all aspects of the company, including branding, marketing, and employee communication

By establishing a clear mission, vision, and values, you can create a shared sense of purpose and direction that supports a growth-oriented culture.

Foster a Culture of Learning and Development

Fostering a culture of learning and development is essential for cultivating a growth-oriented company culture. A culture of learning and development values continuous improvement and encourages employees to seek out new skills and knowledge. Some tips for fostering a culture of learning and development include:

Offering training and development programs that are relevant to employees' skills and experience

Providing opportunities for employees to attend conferences and industry events

Encouraging employees to pursue additional certifications or degrees

Providing mentoring and coaching programs to help employees develop their skills and advance their careers

By fostering a culture of learning and development, you can create a growth-oriented culture that values continuous improvement and supports employee development.

Encourage Innovation and Creativity

Encouraging innovation and creativity is essential for creating a growth-oriented company culture. An innovative and creative culture values new ideas and approaches, and encourages employees to think outside the box. Some tips for encouraging innovation and creativity include:

> ➤ Providing opportunities for brainstorming and idea sharing
> ➤ Creating a culture that values risk-taking and experimentation
> ➤ Encouraging employees to challenge assumptions and explore new ideas
> ➤ Providing resources and support for employees to pursue new initiatives and projects

Create a Positive Work Environment

Creating a positive work environment is essential for cultivating a growth-oriented company culture. A positive work environment values employee satisfaction and engagement, and supports employee well-being. Some tips for creating a positive work environment include:

➤ Encouraging open communication and collaboration among team members

➤ Offering opportunities for team-building and social events

➤ Providing regular feedback and recognition for good performance

➤ Encouraging employee development and professional growth

Prioritize Diversity and Inclusion

Prioritizing diversity and inclusion is essential for cultivating a growth-oriented company culture. A diverse and inclusive culture values different perspectives and experiences, and encourages employees to bring their whole selves to work. Some tips for prioritizing diversity and inclusion include:

➤ Providing diversity and inclusion training for all employees

➤ Actively recruiting and retaining a diverse workforce

➤ Creating a culture that values and celebrates different perspectives and experiences

➤ Providing accommodations and support for employees with diverse backgrounds and needs

Embrace Change and Adaptability

Embracing change and adaptability is essential for cultivating a growth-oriented company culture. A culture that values change and adapt ability is able to quickly respond to changing market conditions and customer needs. Some tips for embracing change and adaptability include:

Encouraging employees to be flexible and adaptable in their approach to work

Creating a culture that values experimentation and risk-taking

Providing resources and support for employees to pursue new initiatives and projects

Communicating changes in the market and industry to all employees

Recognize and Reward Performance

Recognizing and rewarding performance is essential for cultivating a growth-oriented company culture. A culture that values performance recognition and rewards encourages employees to strive for excellence and supports employee motivation. Some tips for recognizing and rewarding performance include:

Providing regular feedback and recognition for good performance

Offering opportunities for bonuses and incentives based on performance and company success

Creating a culture that values and celebrates achievements

Encouraging employees to set and achieve challenging goals

Lead by Example

Leading by example is essential for cultivating a growth-oriented company culture. As a leader, your behavior and actions set the tone for the entire organization. Some tips for leading by example include:

Modeling the behaviors and values that are important to the organization

Communicating regularly and transparently with all employees

Encouraging open communication and collaboration among team members

Providing resources and support for employee development and well-being

Investing in employee development and training

Investing in employee development and training is essential for businesses that want to achieve long-term success. Providing employees with the opportunity to develop their skills and knowledge not only benefits the individual employee, but also benefits the organization as a whole. In this article, we will discuss the key elements of investing in employee development and training.

Identify the Skills and Knowledge Needed

The first step in investing in employee development and training is to identify the skills and knowledge needed for the organization. Some tips for identifying the skills and knowledge needed include:

Conducting a skills gap analysis to identify the areas where employees need improvement

Reviewing the job descriptions and identifying the skills and knowledge required for success in each role

Consulting with managers and team leaders to identify the skills and knowledge needed for their teams

Keeping up to date with industry trends and advancements to identify the skills and knowledge that will be needed in the future

Develop a Comprehensive Training Plan

Developing a comprehensive training plan is essential for investing in employee development and training. A comprehensive training plan outlines the skills and knowledge that employees need to develop, the training programs that will be offered, and the timeline for implementation. Some tips for developing a comprehensive training plan include:

Identifying the most effective training methods for each skill or knowledge area

Outlining the timeline for training implementation and scheduling the necessary resources

Identifying the budget required for training and allocating resources accordingly

Developing a plan for measuring the effectiveness of the training programs

Provide Opportunities for On-The-Job Learning

Providing opportunities for on-the-job learning is essential for investing in employee development and training. On-the-job learning allows employees to develop their skills and knowledge through practical application and experience. Some tips for providing opportunities for on-the-job learning include:

Assigning challenging projects that require employees to develop new skills or knowledge

Providing mentoring and coaching programs to help employees develop their skills and advance their careers

Encouraging employees to take on new responsibilities and learn from their experiences

Providing opportunities for employees to attend conferences and industry events

By providing opportunities for on-the-job learning, you can help employees develop their skills and knowledge in a practical, hands-on environment.

Offer Formal Training Programs

Offering formal training programs is essential for investing in employee development and training. Formal training programs provide employees with structured learning opportunities that are designed to meet specific skill or knowledge gaps. Some tips for offering formal training programs include:

Providing access to training resources such as online courses, workshops, and seminars

Creating a training program that is tailored to the needs of the organization and its employees

Offering certification programs that provide employees with recognized credentials in their field

Providing incentives such as bonuses or promotions for completing training programs

By offering formal training programs, you can help employees develop their skills and knowledge in a structured and comprehensive way.

Provide Opportunities for Career Development

Providing opportunities for career development is essential for investing in employee development and training. Career development opportunities allow employees to advance their careers within the organization and develop new skills and knowledge. Some tips for providing opportunities for career development include:

Providing opportunities for job shadowing or cross-functional training

Offering leadership development programs for employees who want to advance into management roles

Creating a career development plan for each employee that outlines their career goals and the steps needed to achieve them

Encouraging employees to pursue additional certifications or degrees

By providing opportunities for career development, you can help employees advance their careers within the organization and develop the skills and knowledge needed to support their professional growth.

Encourage Continuous Learning

Encouraging continuous learning is essential for investing in employee development and training. Continuous learning allows employees to stay up to date with the latest trends and advancements in their field, and to continually improve their skills and knowledge. Some tips for encouraging continuous learning include:

Providing access to online learning resources such as webinars, podcasts, and articles

Encouraging employees to attend conferences and industry events

Providing opportunities for employees to network with other professionals in their field

Encouraging employees to share their knowledge and expertise with others in the organization

By encouraging continuous learning, you can create a culture of learning and development that supports employee growth and success.

Measure the Effectiveness of Training Programs

Measuring the effectiveness of training programs is essential for investing in employee development and training. By measuring the effectiveness of training programs, you can ensure that your training programs are meeting the needs of the organization and its employees, and adjust the programs as needed. Some tips for measuring the effectiveness of training programs include:

Setting clear objectives and goals for each training program

Evaluating employee performance before and after the training program to measure the impact of the training

Gathering feedback from employees about the effectiveness of the training program

Conducting regular reviews of the training program to identify areas for improvement

By measuring the effectiveness of training programs, you can ensure that your investment in employee development and training is delivering the desired results.

CHAPTER 9

STRATEGIC FINANCIAL MANAGEMENT

Strategic financial management (SFM) plays an essential role in the overall success and longevity of a business. By effectively monitoring and controlling expenses, and ensuring adequate cash flow for expansion, companies can sustain growth, maximize profitability, and maintain a competitive edge. This chapter will discuss the importance of these two critical aspects of SFM and provide insights into how businesses can implement effective strategies to achieve their financial goals.

Monitoring and Controlling Expenses

A key component of SFM is to monitor and control expenses to optimize profitability. By keeping a close eye on expenditures, businesses can identify inefficiencies and areas for cost reduction, ultimately leading to improved financial performance. To effectively monitor and control expenses, companies should consider the following strategies:

Budgeting and Forecasting: Preparing a detailed budget and financial forecast can help businesses anticipate expenses, identify potential cost-saving opportunities, and allocate resources efficiently. Regularly reviewing and updating these financial plans allows for adjustments to be made, ensuring that the company remains on track to achieve its financial goals.

Cost Allocation: Implementing a cost allocation system enables businesses to identify the true cost of each product or service they offer. By understanding the direct and indirect costs associated with each offering, companies can make informed decisions about pricing, resource allocation, and cost reduction initiatives.

Implementing Expense Control Measures: By implementing strict expense control measures, businesses can ensure that all costs are properly reviewed and approved before being incurred. Examples of expense control measures include setting spending limits, requiring management approval for large expenditures, and implementing a centralized procurement process.

Regular Financial Reporting: Regular financial reporting can help businesses track their expenses in real-time and identify any variances from their budget. By monitoring these variances and taking corrective action when necessary, companies can maintain control over their expenses and ensure they are in line with financial expectations.

Benchmarking: Comparing a company's expenses to industry benchmarks can provide valuable insights into areas of potential cost savings. By identifying areas where a business is spending more than its competitors, management can target these areas for cost reduction initiatives.

Ensuring Adequate Cash Flow for Business Expansion

Adequate cash flow is crucial for a business's ability to invest in growth and expansion opportunities. Companies that effectively manage their cash flow can take advantage of strategic investment opportunities, weather economic downturns, and maintain a healthy financial position. To ensure adequate cash flow for business expansion, consider the following strategies:

Cash Flow Forecasting: Developing a cash flow forecast can help businesses anticipate their future cash needs and identify potential cash flow issues before they arise. A cash flow forecast should include all expected inflows and outflows of cash and be updated regularly to reflect changes in business conditions.

Working Capital Management: Effective working capital management involves balancing a company's short-term assets and liabilities to maintain sufficient liquidity for daily operations and growth opportunities. Strategies for improving working capital management include optimizing inventory levels, shortening accounts receivable collection cycles, and extending accounts payable payment terms.

Capital Structure Optimization: Companies can optimize their capital structure by balancing their mix of debt and equity financing. Maintaining an optimal capital structure can help businesses reduce financing costs, maximize cash flow, and provide access to the necessary funds for growth opportunities.

Cash Flow Management Techniques: Implementing cash flow management techniques can help businesses maintain a healthy cash position. Examples of cash flow management techniques include offering early payment discounts to customers, negotiating better payment terms with suppliers, and utilizing a line of credit to manage temporary cash shortfalls.

Monitoring Cash Flow Metrics: Regularly monitoring cash flow metrics, such as the cash conversion cycle and operating cash flow ratio, can provide businesses with valuable insights into their

Cash flow performance. By keeping a close eye on these metrics, companies can identify areas for improvement and take corrective action to ensure they maintain adequate cash flow for expansion.

Investing in Growth Opportunities: When a company has ensured adequate cash flow, it can confidently invest in growth opportunities such as launching new products, expanding into new markets, or acquiring other businesses. These strategic investments can drive long-term revenue growth and create a competitive advantage, ultimately contributing to the overall success of the business.

CHAPTER 10

DATA-DRIVEN DECISION MAKING

In today's data-driven world, businesses can no longer rely solely on intuition or gut feelings to make important decisions. Instead, they must harness the power of data to identify trends, make informed choices, and continuously refine their growth strategies. Data-driven decision-making (DDD) enables companies to become more agile, efficient, and competitive in the ever-evolving business landscape. This chapter will explore the benefits of DDD, provide guidance on how to effectively utilize data for decision-making, and discuss strategies for refining growth based on data insights.

The Importance of Data-Driven Decision-Making

Data-driven decision-making is crucial for businesses to thrive in today's competitive and rapidly changing environment. By using data to inform decisions, companies can:

Make better-informed choices: Data provides objective insights into business performance, market trends, and customer behavior, enabling companies to make well-informed decisions that drive growth and profitability.

Identify opportunities and risks: Analyzing data can help businesses identify emerging trends, growth opportunities, and potential risks, allowing them to take proactive measures to capitalize on opportunities and mitigate risks.

Improve efficiency and agility: DDD enables businesses to identify inefficiencies and optimize processes, leading to increased productivity and reduced costs. Additionally, data-driven organizations can quickly adapt to changes in the market, giving them a competitive advantage.

Enhance customer experiences: By leveraging data to gain insights into customer preferences and behaviors, businesses can create more targeted and personalized offerings, improving customer satisfaction and loyalty.

Utilizing Data to Identify Trends and Make Informed Decisions

To effectively leverage data for decision-making, businesses should consider the following strategies:

Establish clear objectives: Before collecting and analyzing data, businesses must have a clear understanding of their objectives and the specific decisions they need to make. This will ensure that the data collected is relevant and useful for informing these decisions.

Collect and clean data: Companies should gather data from various sources, such as sales, marketing, finance, and customer service, to create a comprehensive view of their business performance. Ensuring that this data is clean and accurate is crucial for reliable decision-making.

Develop analytical skills: Businesses should invest in building their team's analytical skills or partner with external experts to effectively analyze and interpret data. Utilizing advanced analytical techniques, such as predictive modeling and machine learning, can provide valuable insights and support decision-making.

Create data visualizations: Data visualizations can help businesses communicate complex data in a simple and easily digestible format, enabling decision-makers to identify trends and patterns quickly. Examples of data visualizations include bar charts, pie charts, and heat maps.

Foster a data-driven culture: Encouraging a data-driven culture within an organization is critical for the success of DDD. This includes promoting transparency, collaboration, and continuous learning, as well as rewarding employees for data-driven decision-making.

Continuously Refining Growth Strategy Based on Data Insights

Once a business has started utilizing data for decision-making, it is essential to continuously refine its growth strategy based on data insights. The following strategies can help companies achieve this:

Monitor key performance indicators (KPIs): Businesses should identify and track KPIs that are aligned with their strategic objectives. Regularly monitoring these KPIs will enable companies to evaluate the effectiveness of their growth strategy and make data-driven adjustments when necessary.

Conduct regular data audits: Regularly auditing data sources, processes, and systems will ensure that businesses continue to collect high-quality data and maintain the accuracy of their insights.

Encourage experimentation: Fostering a culture of experimentation can help businesses test new ideas, identify best practices, and continuously improve their growth strategies. By conducting controlled experiments and analyzing the results, companies can make data-driven decisions on which initiatives to pursue or refine.

Adapt to changing market conditions: As market conditions evolve, businesses must be prepared to adjust their growth strategies accordingly. By continuously monitoring and analyzing data, companies can identify emerging trends and shifts in consumer behavior, allowing them to adapt and maintain a competitive edge.

Implement feedback loops: Establishing feedback loops within the organization can help businesses continuously learn from their data-driven initiatives. By regularly reviewing the outcomes of data-driven decisions and identifying areas for improvement, companies can refine their strategies and drive continuous growth.

Leverage predictive analytics: Utilizing predictive analytics can help businesses anticipate future trends, customer needs, and market conditions, enabling them to make proactive, data-driven decisions that drive growth.

Data-driven decision-making is essential for businesses to succeed in today's competitive and rapidly changing environment. By effectively utilizing data to identify trends, make informed choices, and continuously refine growth strategies, companies can improve their overall performance, optimize processes, and create a competitive advantage in the market.

Implementing the strategies discussed in this chapter can help businesses harness the power of data and transform it into actionable insights that drive growth and profitability. By fostering a data-driven culture and continuously refining their strategies based on data insights, companies can ensure they are well-positioned to thrive in today's data-driven business landscape.

CHAPTER 11

INNOVATION AND CREATIVITY

Innovation and creativity are essential drivers of success in today's rapidly evolving business landscape. They enable companies to develop novel products and services, solve complex problems, and maintain a competitive edge in the face of ever-changing market conditions. In this chapter, we will explore the importance of innovation and creativity, discuss strategies for identifying opportunities for product and service improvements, and provide guidance on leveraging creative problem-solving techniques.

The Importance of Innovation and Creativity

Innovation and creativity are crucial for businesses to adapt to the dynamic nature of today's markets and remain competitive. By embracing these principles, companies can:

Drive growth: Innovative products and services can generate new revenue streams, expand market share, and create a competitive advantage.

Enhance customer experiences: By creatively addressing customer needs and expectations, businesses can improve customer satisfaction, loyalty, and advocacy.

Increase efficiency: Creative problem-solving can lead to process improvements and cost reductions, enabling businesses to operate more efficiently and profitably.

Foster a culture of continuous improvement: By encouraging innovation and creativity, companies can create a culture that embraces change, adapts to new challenges, and continuously seeks opportunities for growth and improvement.

Identifying Opportunities for Product/Service Improvements

To stay ahead of the competition, businesses must continuously look for opportunities to enhance their products and services. The following strategies can help companies identify these opportunities:

Monitor customer feedback: Actively soliciting and analyzing customer feedback can provide valuable insights into areas where products or services can be improved. This feedback can come from various sources, such as surveys, social media, and customer service interactions.

Analyze market trends: Regularly assessing market trends and competitor offerings can help businesses identify gaps in their product/service offerings and uncover opportunities for improvement.

Conduct internal audits: Regularly evaluating internal processes, systems, and capabilities can reveal inefficiencies and areas for improvement within the organization.

Foster collaboration and ideation: Encouraging cross-functional collaboration and open communication can lead to the generation of new ideas and the identification of opportunities for product/service enhancements.

Experiment with new technologies: Exploring emerging technologies and their potential applications can help businesses uncover innovative ways to improve their products and services.

Leveraging Creative Problem-Solving Techniques

Creative problem-solving techniques can help businesses address complex challenges and generate innovative solutions. The following approaches can be employed to foster creativity and enhance problem-solving capabilities within an organization:

Brainstorming: Brainstorming sessions can help teams generate a diverse range of ideas and potential solutions. Encouraging open dialogue and the free flow of ideas, without judgment or criticism, can lead to more innovative and creative outcomes.

Divergent and Convergent Thinking: Divergent thinking involves generating multiple ideas or solutions to a problem, while convergent thinking focuses on narrowing down these ideas to identify the most viable solution. By utilizing both approaches, businesses can stimulate creativity and improve their problem-solving capabilities.

The Six Thinking Hats Technique: This technique, developed by Edward de Bono, involves viewing a problem from six different perspectives (represented by six different colored hats). By systematically considering each perspective, teams can gain a more comprehensive understanding of a problem and develop well-rounded solutions.

Mind Mapping: Mind mapping is a visual technique that can help teams organize and explore ideas. By visually representing ideas and their connections, teams can gain a better understanding of complex problems and identify potential solutions more effectively.

SCAMPER Technique: SCAMPER is an acronym for Substitute, Combine, Adapt, Modify, Put to another use, Eliminate, and Reverse. By applying these prompts to a problem, teams can generate creative ideas and identify new ways to improve products or services.

Design Thinking: Design thinking is a human-centered approach to problem-solving that focuses on understanding the needs and desires of end-users. By empathizing with users, defining problems, ideating solutions, prototyping, and testing, businesses can create innovative products and services that resonate with their target audience.

Encourage a culture of creativity: Fostering a culture that values creativity and innovation can help businesses tap into the full potential of their workforce. This includes providing employees with the necessary resources, time, and support to explore new ideas, take risks, and learn from failures.

Implementing and Scaling Innovative Solutions

Once a creative solution has been identified, businesses must effectively implement and scale these innovations to drive growth and maintain a competitive edge. The following strategies can support the successful implementation and scaling of innovative solutions:

Develop a clear implementation plan: A well-defined implementation plan should outline the objectives, resources, timeline, and key stakeholders involved in bringing the innovation to fruition. This plan can help ensure that all parties are aligned and that the project remains on track.

Establish metrics for success: Defining clear metrics for success can help businesses objectively evaluate the impact of their innovations and make data-driven decisions about scaling and further development.

Foster cross-functional collaboration: Encouraging collaboration between different departments and functions can help ensure that all aspects of the innovation are considered and integrated into the organization's processes and systems.

Communicate and celebrate successes: Sharing and celebrating the successful implementation of innovative solutions can help build momentum and foster a culture of innovation within the organization.

Continuously iterate and improve: Innovation is an ongoing process. Businesses should continuously monitor the performance of their innovations, gather feedback, and make data-driven adjustments to optimize results and drive continuous improvement.

Innovation and creativity are essential for businesses to remain competitive and thrive in today's dynamic market landscape. By actively identifying opportunities for product and service improvements and leveraging creative problem-solving techniques, companies can develop novel solutions that drive growth, enhance customer experiences, and improve overall performance.

Implementing the strategies discussed in this chapter can help businesses foster a culture of innovation and creativity, empowering them to address complex challenges, adapt to changing market conditions, and maintain a competitive edge. By continuously refining their products and services based on customer needs and market trends, companies can position themselves for long-term success in today's rapidly evolving business environment.

CHAPTER 12

EFFECTIVE BUSINESS NETWORKING

In today's interconnected business landscape, effective networking is essential for building valuable relationships, gaining new insights, and uncovering opportunities for growth. Business networking can lead to strategic partnerships, increased sales, and a greater understanding of industry trends. This chapter will discuss the importance of business networking, provide guidance on developing a successful networking strategy, and offer tips for nurturing and maintaining professional relationships.

The Importance of Business Networking

Business networking can provide a multitude of benefits, including:

Access to new opportunities: Networking can help businesses uncover potential clients, suppliers, investors, and partners, leading to increased sales and improved operations.

Knowledge and information sharing: Interacting with professionals from various industries can provide insights into market trends, best practices, and emerging technologies, enabling businesses to stay informed and competitive.

Increased visibility and credibility: Building a strong professional network can help raise a business's profile, enhance its reputation, and foster trust among potential clients and partners.

Personal and professional development: Networking can lead to mentorship opportunities, skills development, and career advancement for individuals within an organization.

Support and advice: A robust professional network can provide valuable support and guidance when facing challenges or making strategic decisions.

Developing a Successful Networking Strategy

To maximize the benefits of business networking, it is essential to develop a targeted and purposeful strategy. The following steps can help guide the development of a successful networking plan:

Define objectives: Clearly outline the goals of your networking efforts, such as expanding your client base, finding potential partners, or staying informed about industry trends. This will help guide your networking activities and ensure they are aligned with your overall business objectives.

Identify target contacts: Research and compile a list of professionals and organizations that align with your networking goals. This can include industry leaders, potential clients or partners, and influential individuals within your field.

Choose the right networking events and platforms: Select networking events, conferences, and online platforms that cater to your target audience and provide opportunities for meaningful interactions. This can include industry-specific events, local business groups, or professional social media platforms such as LinkedIn.

Develop a personal brand: Create a consistent and professional image across all networking channels, including business cards, social media profiles, and personal interactions. This will help establish credibility and make a lasting impression on potential contacts.

Prepare an elevator pitch: Develop a concise and compelling summary of your business and its value proposition. This will enable you to quickly communicate your key message and spark interest during networking interactions.

Tips for Effective Networking

Implementing the following tips can help enhance the effectiveness of your networking efforts:

Be genuine and authentic: Approach networking with sincerity and a genuine interest in others. This will help build trust and foster meaningful relationships.

Listen actively: Focus on truly understanding the needs, interests, and concerns of your networking contacts. This will enable you to identify potential opportunities for collaboration and demonstrate your value as a resource.

Ask open-ended questions: Encourage deeper conversations by asking open-ended questions that prompt thoughtful responses. This can help you gain valuable insights and build rapport with your contacts.

Offer value: Seek opportunities to provide value to your networking contacts, such as sharing relevant information, making introductions, or offering assistance with a challenge. This will help establish you as a valuable resource and strengthen your professional relationships.

Follow up and stay connected: Maintain regular contact with your networking connections through email, social media, or in-person meetings. This will help nurture relationships, keep you top of mind, and increase the likelihood of uncovering new opportunities.

Maintain a positive attitude: Approach networking with enthusiasm and a positive mindset. This will help you make a strong impression, build rapport, and foster lasting connections with your contacts.

Practice good time management: Be mindful of your time and the time of others during networking interactions. This will help ensure that conversations are productive and respectful of each party's schedule.

Be open to learning: Embrace the opportunity to learn from others during networking interactions. This can help broaden your perspective, enhance your skills, and contribute to your personal and professional growth.

Develop your communication skills: Effective communication is crucial for successful networking. Work on honing your listening, speaking, and interpersonal skills to maximize the impact of your networking efforts.

Leverage technology: Utilize digital tools and platforms to support your networking efforts, such as social media, email marketing, and virtual events. This can help you stay connected with your network and expand your reach beyond in-person interactions.

Nurturing and Maintaining Professional Relationships

Building and nurturing professional relationships is critical for long-term networking success. The following strategies can help maintain and strengthen your professional connections:

Be consistent and reliable: Demonstrate your commitment to your professional relationships by consistently delivering on promises, meeting deadlines, and maintaining open lines of communication.

Show appreciation: Regularly express gratitude and appreciation to your networking contacts for their support, advice, and collaboration. This can help reinforce your connections and create a sense of mutual respect.

Offer support: Be proactive in offering assistance, guidance, or resources to your contacts when they face challenges or seek opportunities for growth. This will help reinforce your value as a trusted resource within your network.

Celebrate successes: Share and celebrate the achievements of your networking contacts. This can help foster a sense of camaraderie and create positive associations with your professional relationships.

Continuously invest in your network: Dedicate time and effort to regularly engage with your professional contacts, attend networking events, and expand your network. This will help ensure that your networking efforts remain productive and beneficial in the long term.

Effective business networking is essential for establishing valuable relationships, uncovering new opportunities, and staying informed about industry trends. By developing a targeted networking strategy, leveraging key networking tips, and nurturing professional relationships, businesses can maximize the benefits of their networking efforts and drive success in today's interconnected business landscape. Implementing the strategies discussed in this chapter can help businesses create a robust and impactful professional network that supports their growth and long-term success.

CHAPTER 13

MASTERING THE ART OF SALES

In any business, sales play a critical role in driving growth, generating revenue, and ensuring long-term success. Mastering the art of sales involves developing a deep understanding of customer needs, effectively communicating the value of your product or service, and building lasting relationships. This chapter will discuss the importance of sales in business, outline key principles for successful selling, and provide guidance on refining your sales strategy.

The Importance of Sales in Business

Sales are essential for the success of any business, as they directly impact revenue generation, customer acquisition, and market penetration. By mastering the art of sales, businesses can:

Drive growth: Effective sales strategies can help businesses acquire new customers, increase market share, and drive revenue growth.

Enhance customer experiences: By understanding customer needs and preferences, sales professionals can provide personalized solutions that improve customer satisfaction and loyalty.

Foster long-term relationships: Building strong relationships with customers can lead to repeat business, referrals, and an enhanced reputation in the market.

Gain a competitive advantage: Developing superior sales skills and strategies can help businesses differentiate themselves from competitors and capture a larger share of the market.

Key Principles for Successful Selling

The following principles can help guide the development of effective sales strategies and tactics:

Understand your customer: Develop a deep understanding of your target audience, including their needs, pain points, preferences, and decision-making processes. This will enable you to tailor your sales approach and offer relevant, personalized solutions.

Focus on value: Clearly articulate the value proposition of your product or service, highlighting how it addresses customer needs, provides benefits, and offers a return on investment. This will help customers understand the tangible advantages of choosing your offering over competitors.

Build rapport and trust: Establishing a genuine connection with customers and demonstrating empathy can help build trust and foster long-term relationships. This involves active listening, asking open-ended questions, and showcasing genuine interest in the customer's situation.

Develop effective communication skills: Strong communication skills are essential for successful selling. This includes clear and concise messaging, persuasive storytelling, and the ability to adapt your communication style to suit the needs of individual customers.

Leverage sales tools and technology: Utilize sales tools and technologies, such as customer relationship management (CRM) systems, sales automation software, and data analytics, to enhance your sales processes, improve efficiency, and gain insights into customer behavior.

Refining Your Sales Strategy

Developing a successful sales strategy involves continuous evaluation, adaptation, and improvement. The following steps can help businesses refine their sales strategies and drive better results:

Set clear goals and objectives: Establish specific, measurable, achievable, relevant, and time-bound (SMART) sales goals and objectives that align with your overall business strategy. This will provide a clear direction for your sales efforts and enable you to track progress and measure success.

Analyze and segment your target market: Conduct market research to gain insights into your target audience and segment your market based on factors such as demographics, psychographics, and customer needs. This will enable you to develop targeted sales approaches and messaging that resonate with each segment.

Develop a sales process: Create a structured sales process that outlines the key steps involved in moving a prospect from initial contact to closed sale. This can help ensure consistency, improve efficiency, and enable you to identify areas for improvement.

Train and develop your sales team: Invest in ongoing training and development for your sales team, focusing on areas such as product knowledge, communication skills, and sales techniques. This will help enhance their performance and drive better results.

Monitor and evaluate performance: Regularly review your sales performance, analyzing key metrics and identifying areas for improvement. This can involve conducting regular sales meetings, tracking performance against goals, and evaluating the effectiveness of sales strategies and tactics.

Adapt and optimize: Continuously refine and optimize your sales strategy based on performance data, market trends, and customer feedback. This can involve adjusting your target market segments, revising your sales process, or implementing new sales techniques and technologies.

Foster a sales-driven culture: Encourage a culture that values and supports sales excellence within your organization. This includes recognizing and rewarding high-performing sales team members, promoting collaboration and knowledge sharing, and emphasizing the importance of sales to overall business success.

Overcoming Sales Challenges

Sales professionals often face a variety of challenges, such as dealing with objections, navigating competitive markets, and managing rejection. The following strategies can help overcome these challenges and drive sales success:

Develop resilience and perseverance: Cultivate a resilient mindset and the ability to persevere through setbacks and rejection. This involves maintaining a positive attitude, learning from failures, and staying focused on your long-term goals.

Master the art of handling objections: Develop techniques for effectively addressing and overcoming customer objections. This includes actively listening to customer concerns, providing well-reasoned responses, and offering alternative solutions when necessary.

Differentiate your offering: Identify and communicate the unique selling points of your product or service, focusing on the aspects that set you apart from competitors. This can help you stand out in crowded markets and appeal to customers seeking a distinctive solution.

Leverage customer testimonials and case studies: Showcase the success of your existing customers through testimonials and case studies. This can help build credibility, demonstrate the real-world benefits of your product or service, and provide social proof to potential customers.

Continuously expand your network: Develop and maintain a broad professional network that can help generate leads, provide referrals, and offer valuable insights into market trends and opportunities.

Mastering the art of sales is essential for driving business growth, enhancing customer experiences, and establishing long-term relationships. By understanding key principles for successful selling, refining your sales strategy, and overcoming common challenges, businesses can unlock the full potential of their sales efforts and drive success in today's competitive market landscape. Implementing the strategies discussed in this chapter can help businesses develop a high-performing sales team, deliver exceptional customer value, and achieve lasting success in the marketplace.

CHAPTER 14

BUSINESS GROWTH THROUGH ACQUISITIONS AND MERGERS

In today's competitive business environment, achieving sustainable growth is a top priority for many organizations. Acquisitions and mergers offer businesses the opportunity to expand their market share, enhance their product or service offerings, and realize synergies that drive increased efficiency and profitability. This chapter will discuss the benefits of mergers and acquisitions, outline key considerations for successful transactions, and provide guidance on managing the integration process.

The Benefits of Mergers and Acquisitions

Mergers and acquisitions can provide a range of benefits for businesses, including:

Increased market share: Acquiring or merging with a competitor can help businesses expand their customer base and increase their market share, positioning them for greater long-term success.

Diversification: Mergers and acquisitions can enable businesses to diversify their product or service offerings, reducing risk and increasing revenue potential.

Access to new markets and customers: Acquiring or merging with a company that operates in a different geographic region or market segment can help businesses tap into new growth opportunities and customer segments.

Synergies and cost savings: Combining operations, resources, and technologies can lead to significant cost savings and operational efficiencies, driving increased profitability and competitiveness.

Access to new technologies and intellectual property: Acquiring or merging with a company that possesses innovative technologies or intellectual property can help businesses enhance their capabilities, differentiate their offerings, and stay ahead of the competition.

Talent acquisition: Mergers and acquisitions can provide access to experienced and skilled employees, strengthening a business's human capital and enhancing its overall performance.

Key Considerations for Successful Mergers and Acquisitions

To maximize the benefits of mergers and acquisitions, businesses should carefully consider the following factors:

Strategic alignment: Ensure that the target company aligns with your overall business strategy and growth objectives. This includes assessing factors such as market position, product or service offerings, and potential synergies.

Cultural fit: Evaluate the compatibility of the two organizations' cultures, values, and management styles. A strong cultural fit can help facilitate a smoother integration process and minimize potential conflicts.

Financial analysis: Conduct thorough financial due diligence to assess the target company's financial health, performance, and potential risks. This includes analyzing factors such as revenue, profitability, cash flow, and debt levels.

Valuation: Develop a comprehensive valuation model to determine the appropriate price for the target company, taking into account factors such as future cash flows, growth potential, and risk.

Deal structure: Carefully consider the structure of the transaction, such as whether it will be a stock or asset purchase, and the financing options available. This can impact the tax implications, legal liabilities, and overall cost of the transaction.

Regulatory compliance: Ensure that the transaction complies with all applicable laws and regulations, such as antitrust laws, industry-specific regulations, and foreign investment restrictions.

Managing the Integration Process

The integration process is a critical component of a successful merger or acquisition. The following steps can help guide the integration process and ensure a smooth transition:

Develop a clear integration plan: Establish a detailed plan outlining the objectives, timeline, resources, and key stakeholders involved in the integration process. This can help ensure that all parties are aligned and that the process remains on track.

Communicate effectively: Clearly communicate the rationale for the transaction, the benefits for both organizations, and the expected outcomes to all stakeholders, including employees, customers, and investors. This can help build support for the integration and minimize uncertainty.

Assign integration teams: Designate cross-functional integration teams, comprising members from both organizations, to oversee specific aspects of the integration, such as operations, technology, and human resources.

Establish performance metrics: Define key performance indicators (KPIs) to monitor and measure the success of the integration process. This can help ensure that the integration remains on track, and any potential issues are promptly addressed.

Preserve company culture and values: Work to maintain and integrate the unique cultures and values of both organizations, fostering a sense of unity and collaboration among employees. This can help reduce potential conflicts and enhance employee engagement during the integration process.

Integrate systems and processes: Assess and consolidate systems and processes, such as IT infrastructure, financial reporting, and supply chain management. This can help realize synergies, improve efficiency, and provide a consistent experience for customers and employees.

Address talent management and retention: Proactively address talent management issues, such as employee retention, compensation, and career development, to ensure a smooth transition and maintain a skilled, motivated workforce.

Continuously evaluate and adjust: Regularly assess the progress of the integration process, identifying areas for improvement and adjusting the integration plan as needed. This can help ensure that the integration remains on track and that any potential issues are promptly addressed.

Mergers and acquisitions offer significant potential for business growth, providing access to new markets, customers, technologies, and talent. However, to maximize the benefits of these transactions, businesses must carefully consider key factors such as strategic alignment, cultural fit, financial analysis, and deal structure. By effectively managing the integration process and addressing potential challenges, businesses can realize the full potential of mergers and acquisitions, driving increased efficiency, competitiveness, and long-term success. Implementing the strategies discussed in this chapter can help businesses navigate the complex world of mergers and acquisitions, and achieve sustainable growth in today's dynamic business environment.

CHAPTER 15

UTILIZING TECHNOLOGY FOR COMPETITIVE ADVANTAGE

In today's rapidly evolving business landscape, technology plays a critical role in enabling organizations to stay ahead of the competition and drive innovation, efficiency, and growth. Leveraging the power of technology can provide businesses with a competitive advantage by improving customer experiences, enhancing operational capabilities, and facilitating data-driven decision-making. This chapter will discuss the importance of utilizing technology for competitive advantage, explore key technological trends and tools, and provide guidance on incorporating technology into your business strategy.

The Importance of Technology for Competitive Advantage

Embracing technology and incorporating it into various aspects of a business can provide a range of benefits, including:

Increased efficiency: Technology can help automate repetitive tasks, streamline processes, and reduce human error, leading to increased efficiency and productivity.

Improved decision-making: Data-driven technologies can provide businesses with valuable insights and analytics, enabling more informed and strategic decision-making.

Enhanced customer experiences: Technology can help businesses better understand customer needs and preferences, deliver personalized experiences, and improve customer satisfaction and loyalty.

Innovation and differentiation: Adopting innovative technologies can help businesses differentiate their product or service offerings, drive innovation, and maintain a competitive edge.

Cost savings: Implementing technology can lead to cost savings by optimizing resource utilization, reducing waste, and improving overall operational efficiency.

Scalability and growth: Leveraging technology can enable businesses to scale more efficiently, accommodate growth, and expand their market reach.

Key Technological Trends and Tools

To stay competitive in today's digital age, businesses must stay informed of emerging technological trends and tools. The following are some key trends and tools that businesses should consider leveraging for competitive advantage:

Cloud computing: Cloud computing allows businesses to store and manage data and applications remotely, providing increased flexibility, scalability, and cost savings. Adopting cloud-based solutions can enable businesses to access advanced infrastructure and services without significant upfront investments.

Internet of Things (IoT): IoT technology connects physical devices, vehicles, and appliances to the internet, enabling real-time data collection and analysis. IoT can help businesses improve operational efficiency, enhance product offerings, and create new revenue streams.

Big data analytics: Big data analytics involves processing and analyzing large volumes of data to uncover patterns, trends, and insights that can inform business decisions. Leveraging big data analytics can help businesses identify new opportunities, optimize operations, and better understand customer behavior.

Blockchain technology: Blockchain is a decentralized, distributed ledger technology that can help businesses improve transparency, security, and efficiency in various applications, such as supply chain management, financial transactions, and data storage.

Cybersecurity: As businesses become increasingly reliant on digital technologies, ensuring the security and integrity of data and systems is paramount. Implementing robust cybersecurity measures can help protect businesses from threats, safeguard customer information, and maintain trust in the digital age.

Incorporating Technology into Your Business Strategy

To effectively leverage technology for competitive advantage, businesses must develop a comprehensive technology strategy that aligns with their overall business objectives. The following steps can help guide the development and implementation of a technology strategy:

Assess your current technology landscape: Evaluate your existing technology infrastructure, systems, and processes to identify strengths, weaknesses, and opportunities for improvement. This includes considering factors such as data storage, security, and system integration.

Define your technology objectives: Establish clear objectives for your technology strategy, ensuring alignment with your overall business goals and objectives. This may involve improving operational efficiency, enhancing customer experiences, or driving innovation and differentiation in your product or service offerings.

Identify relevant technological trends and tools: Research and analyze emerging technological trends and tools that align with your business objectives and have the potential to deliver a competitive advantage. Consider factors such as cost, scalability, and ease of implementation.

Develop a technology roadmap: Create a technology roadmap outlining the specific tools and solutions you plan to implement, along with a timeline and milestones for achieving your technology objectives. This roadmap should be regularly updated to reflect changes in your business environment, objectives, and technological landscape.

Allocate resources and investment: Allocate appropriate financial and human resources to support the implementation of your technology strategy. This may involve hiring or training employees with the necessary skills, investing in hardware or software, or partnering with external technology providers.

Implement and monitor: Execute your technology roadmap, closely monitoring progress against your objectives and adjusting your strategy as needed based on performance and changing circumstances. Regularly review the effectiveness of your technology investments and ensure that they continue to deliver value and support your business objectives.

Foster a culture of innovation and technology adoption: Encourage a culture that embraces technological innovation and adoption across all levels of your organization. This includes providing ongoing training and development opportunities, recognizing and rewarding technology-driven achievements, and promoting collaboration and knowledge sharing.

Ensure data security and privacy: Implement robust data security and privacy measures to protect your organization and customers from potential threats, and to comply with relevant regulations and industry standards.

Utilizing technology for competitive advantage is essential for businesses to succeed in today's digital age. By staying informed of emerging technological trends, incorporating technology into your business strategy, and fostering a culture of innovation and technology adoption, businesses can drive efficiency, enhance customer experiences, and differentiate themselves in the market. Implementing the strategies discussed in this chapter can help businesses navigate the complexities of the digital landscape, harness the power of technology, and achieve lasting success in an increasingly competitive environment.

CHAPTER 16

IMPLEMENTING EFFICIENT OPERATIONS MANAGEMENT

Efficient operations management is a vital component of a successful business, as it encompasses the processes and practices involved in planning, organizing, and overseeing the production and delivery of goods and services. By implementing efficient operations management, businesses can reduce costs, improve quality, enhance customer satisfaction, and drive growth. This chapter will discuss the importance of operations management, explore key principles and techniques, and provide guidance on implementing effective operations management strategies.

The Importance of Operations Management

Effective operations management is essential for businesses to achieve their objectives and remain competitive in today's dynamic market. Some of the key benefits of efficient operations management include:

Cost reduction: By optimizing processes, eliminating waste, and improving resource utilization, businesses can reduce operational costs and enhance profitability.

Improved quality: Effective operations management can help businesses improve the quality of their products and services by implementing rigorous quality control measures, addressing production issues, and fostering a culture of continuous improvement.

Enhanced customer satisfaction: Efficient operations management can enable businesses to deliver products and services more quickly, accurately, and reliably, leading to higher levels of customer satisfaction and loyalty.

Increased competitiveness: By improving efficiency, quality, and customer satisfaction, businesses can gain a competitive edge in the market, positioning themselves for long-term success.

Scalability and growth: Efficient operations management can help businesses scale their operations more effectively, accommodate growth, and expand their market reach.

Key Principles and Techniques in Operations Management

To implement efficient operations management, businesses should adopt a range of principles and techniques that can help optimize processes, improve quality, and drive continuous improvement. Some key principles and techniques include:

Lean management: Lean management is a process improvement methodology that focuses on reducing waste and maximizing value in business operations. Key lean principles include continuous improvement, eliminating non-value-adding activities, and optimizing resource utilization.

Total quality management (TQM): TQM is an approach to operations management that emphasizes continuous improvement, customer satisfaction, and the involvement of all employees in the pursuit of quality. TQM includes techniques such as statistical process control, root cause analysis, and employee training and development.

Six Sigma: Six Sigma is a data-driven methodology for process improvement that aims to reduce defects and variability in business processes. The Six Sigma approach involves identifying and analyzing the root causes of defects, implementing process improvements, and monitoring the results to ensure that improvements are sustained.

Just-in-Time (JIT) production: JIT production is a manufacturing strategy that seeks to minimize inventory levels and reduce lead times by producing goods only when they are needed. This approach can help businesses reduce costs, improve efficiency, and enhance responsiveness to customer needs.

Capacity planning: Capacity planning involves determining the optimal level of resources required to meet demand for products and services. This includes assessing factors such as equipment, labor, and facilities to ensure that businesses can meet customer needs while minimizing costs and maximizing efficiency.

Forecasting and demand management: Accurate forecasting and demand management are essential for effective operations management, as they enable businesses to anticipate customer needs, allocate resources, and plan production schedules more effectively.

Supply chain management: Effective supply chain management involves optimizing the flow of materials, information, and financial resources throughout the entire supply chain, from suppliers to manufacturers, distributors, and customers. This can help businesses reduce costs, improve efficiency, and enhance customer satisfaction.

Implementing Efficient Operations Management Strategies

To implement efficient operations management, businesses should follow a structured approach that includes the following steps:

Assess your current operations: Begin by evaluating your existing operations to identify strengths, weaknesses, and opportunities for improvement. This may involve conducting a thorough review of your processes, systems, and performance metrics.

Define your operations management objectives: Establish clear objectives for your operations management strategy, ensuring alignment with your overall business goals and objectives. This may involve improving efficiency, reducing costs, enhancing quality, or increasing customer satisfaction.

Develop an operations management plan: Create a comprehensive operations management plan that outlines the specific strategies, techniques, and tools you will implement to achieve your objectives. This plan should include timelines, milestones, and performance metrics to track progress and success.

Implement process improvements: Identify and implement process improvements that align with your operations management objectives. This may involve adopting lean management principles, implementing Six Sigma techniques, or optimizing supply chain processes.

Invest in technology and tools: Evaluate and invest in technology and tools that can support your operations management objectives. This may include software for production planning, inventory management, or data analytics, as well as hardware such as automation equipment or advanced manufacturing technologies.

Train and develop employees: Provide ongoing training and development opportunities for employees to ensure they have the skills and knowledge required to support your operations management objectives. This may include training in lean management, Six Sigma, or other relevant methodologies.

Monitor and measure performance: Regularly track and measure the performance of your operations against your objectives, using key performance indicators (KPIs) and other performance metrics. This will enable you to identify areas for improvement, adjust your operations management strategy as needed, and ensure that your efforts are delivering the desired results.

Foster a culture of continuous improvement: Encourage a culture of continuous improvement throughout your organization, empowering employees to identify and implement process improvements, and promoting collaboration and knowledge sharing. This can help drive ongoing efficiency gains and ensure that your operations management strategy remains effective over time.

Implementing efficient operations management is essential for businesses to remain competitive, reduce costs, improve quality, and enhance customer satisfaction. By adopting key principles and techniques such as lean management, Six Sigma, and capacity planning, and following a structured approach to operations management, businesses can optimize their processes and drive sustainable growth. Embracing the strategies discussed in this chapter can help businesses navigate the complexities of operations management, harness the power of continuous improvement, and achieve lasting success in today's dynamic business environment.

CHAPTER 17

RISK MANAGEMENT AND MITIGATION

Risk management is a critical aspect of running a successful business, as it involves the identification, assessment, and mitigation of risks that may impact an organization's objectives, operations, or reputation. By implementing effective risk management and mitigation strategies, businesses can reduce the likelihood and impact of potential threats, enhance decision-making, and protect their long-term viability. This chapter will discuss the importance of risk management and mitigation, explore key concepts and techniques, and provide guidance on implementing a comprehensive risk management framework.

The Importance of Risk Management and Mitigation

Effective risk management and mitigation are essential for businesses to achieve their objectives and maintain a competitive edge in today's dynamic market. Some of the key benefits of risk management and mitigation include:

Improved decision-making: Risk management can help businesses make more informed decisions by identifying potential threats and opportunities, assessing their likelihood and impact, and developing appropriate response strategies.

Enhanced operational efficiency: By identifying and mitigating risks that may disrupt operations, businesses can reduce downtime, minimize costs, and improve overall efficiency.

Protection of assets and reputation: Effective risk management can help businesses protect their physical, financial, and intangible assets, as well as maintain their reputation and customer trust.

Compliance with regulations and standards: Risk management can help businesses ensure compliance with relevant laws, regulations, and industry standards, reducing the potential for fines, penalties, and legal issues.

Greater stakeholder confidence: Implementing robust risk management and mitigation strategies can increase the confidence of stakeholders, including investors, customers, and employees, in the organization's ability to manage challenges and achieve its objectives.

Key Concepts and Techniques in Risk Management and Mitigation

To implement effective risk management and mitigation, businesses should adopt a range of concepts and techniques that can help identify, assess, and address potential risks. Some key concepts and techniques include:

Risk identification: The first step in the risk management process involves identifying potential risks that may impact an organization's objectives, operations, or reputation. This may involve conducting a comprehensive risk assessment, gathering input from stakeholders, and reviewing internal and external data sources.

Risk assessment: Once risks have been identified, businesses should assess their likelihood and potential impact. This may involve using quantitative and qualitative methods, such as scenario analysis, expert judgment, or historical data, to estimate the probability and consequences of each risk.

Risk prioritization: After assessing risks, businesses should prioritize them based on their likelihood and impact, as well as their potential to be managed or mitigated. This can help organizations allocate resources more effectively and focus on the most significant risks.

Risk mitigation: Businesses should develop and implement appropriate strategies to mitigate identified risks, reducing their likelihood or impact. Risk mitigation strategies may include risk avoidance, risk reduction, risk transfer, or risk acceptance, depending on the nature and severity of the risk.

Risk monitoring and review: Regularly monitoring and reviewing risks is an essential component of effective risk management, as it enables businesses to track changes in risk levels, assess the effectiveness of mitigation strategies, and identify emerging risks. This may involve tracking key risk indicators (KRIs), conducting periodic risk assessments, and updating risk registers and mitigation plans as needed.

Risk communication and reporting: Communicating risk information to stakeholders, including employees, management, and investors, is a critical aspect of risk management. This may involve developing risk reports, dashboards, or other communication tools to ensure that stakeholders are informed of the organization's risk profile and mitigation efforts.

Implementing a Comprehensive Risk Management Framework

To implement effective risk management and mitigation, businesses should establish a comprehensive risk management framework that aligns with their objectives and risk appetite. The following steps can guide the development and implementation of a risk management framework:

Establish a risk management policy: Develop a risk management policy that outlines your organization's approach to identifying, assessing, and mitigating risks. This policy should define your risk appetite, establish roles and responsibilities, and provide guidance on the risk management process.

Create a risk management team: Assemble a risk management team with representatives from key areas of your organization, such as finance, operations, and IT. This team should be responsible for overseeing the risk management process, providing expert input, and ensuring that risk management activities are integrated across the organization.

Conduct risk identification and assessment: Implement a structured process for identifying and assessing risks across your organization. This may involve conducting regular risk assessments, gathering input from stakeholders, and reviewing internal and external data sources.

Develop risk mitigation strategies: Based on your risk assessments, develop and implement appropriate risk mitigation strategies to address identified risks. These strategies should be aligned with your organization's risk appetite and overall objectives and should consider the costs and benefits of different risk management approaches.

Establish risk monitoring and review processes: Implement processes to regularly monitor and review your organization's risk profile, the effectiveness of risk mitigation strategies, and emerging risks. This may involve tracking key risk indicators (KRIs), conducting periodic risk assessments, and updating risk registers and mitigation plans as needed.

Communicate and report on risk management activities: Develop communication and reporting mechanisms to ensure that stakeholders, including employees, management, and investors, are informed of your organization's risk management activities. This may involve creating risk reports, dashboards, or other communication tools to provide a clear and consistent view of risk across the organization.

Continuously improve your risk management framework: Regularly review and refine your risk management framework to ensure that it remains effective in managing and mitigating risks. This may involve incorporating lessons learned, adopting best practices, and updating your risk management policy and processes as needed.

Effective risk management and mitigation are essential for businesses to achieve their objectives, protect their assets and reputation, and maintain a competitive edge in today's dynamic market. By adopting key concepts and techniques, such as risk identification, assessment, and prioritization, and implementing a comprehensive risk management framework, businesses can reduce the likelihood and impact of potential threats and enhance their resilience. Implementing the strategies discussed in this chapter can help businesses navigate the complexities of risk management, harness the power of proactive risk mitigation, and achieve lasting success in an increasingly uncertain business environment.

CHAPTER 18

MEASURING AND CELEBRATING SUCCESS

In today's competitive business environment, measuring and celebrating success is crucial for organizations to maintain motivation, foster a sense of accomplishment, and ensure continuous improvement. By establishing clear performance metrics, regularly reviewing progress, and acknowledging achievements, businesses can create a culture of success that drives engagement, productivity, and growth. This chapter will discuss the importance of measuring and celebrating success, explore key concepts and techniques, and provide guidance on developing a comprehensive approach to recognizing and rewarding achievement.

The Importance of Measuring and Celebrating Success

Measuring and celebrating success is essential for businesses to achieve their objectives and maintain a competitive edge in today's dynamic market. Some of the key benefits of measuring and celebrating success include:

Enhanced motivation and engagement: Recognizing and celebrating achievements can boost employee motivation and engagement, fostering a sense of pride and ownership in their work.

Improved performance: By establishing clear performance metrics and regularly reviewing progress, businesses can drive continuous improvement, identify areas for growth, and enhance overall performance.

Increased employee retention: Acknowledging and rewarding success can help businesses retain top talent by fostering a sense of loyalty and commitment, reducing the costs associated with employee turnover.

Strengthened organizational culture: Celebrating success can help businesses create a positive organizational culture that values achievement, collaboration, and innovation, positioning them for long-term success.

Greater stakeholder confidence: Measuring and celebrating success can increase the confidence of stakeholders, including investors, customers, and employees, in the organization's ability to achieve its objectives and deliver value.

Key Concepts and Techniques in Measuring and Celebrating Success

To effectively measure and celebrate success, businesses should adopt a range of concepts and techniques that can help track progress, recognize achievements, and foster a culture of success. Some key concepts and techniques include:

Establishing clear performance metrics: Businesses should establish clear, measurable, and relevant performance metrics that align with their objectives and can be used to assess progress and success. These metrics may include financial indicators, customer satisfaction scores, employee engagement levels, or innovation metrics, depending on the organization's goals and priorities.

Regularly reviewing progress: Businesses should regularly review their progress against established performance metrics to identify areas for improvement, assess the effectiveness of their strategies, and ensure that they are on track to achieve their objectives. This may involve conducting periodic performance reviews, tracking key performance indicators (KPIs), or using data analytics tools to monitor progress.

Recognizing and rewarding achievement: Businesses should develop and implement recognition and reward programs that acknowledge and celebrate individual and team achievements. These programs may include formal recognition events, financial incentives, or non-financial rewards, such as professional development opportunities, time off, or public acknowledgment.

Fostering a culture of success: Businesses should actively promote a culture of success by encouraging collaboration, innovation, and continuous improvement. This may involve providing resources and support for employee development, recognizing and sharing best practices, and creating opportunities for employees to contribute to the organization's success.

Communicating success stories: Businesses should regularly communicate their success stories to stakeholders, including employees, customers, and investors, to maintain motivation, build trust, and reinforce their commitment to achieving their objectives. This may involve sharing success stories in internal and external communications, highlighting achievements on social media, or presenting success stories at industry events.

Developing a Comprehensive Approach to Measuring and Celebrating Success

To develop a comprehensive approach to measuring and celebrating success, businesses should follow a structured process that includes the following steps:

Define success: Begin by defining what success looks like for your organization, ensuring alignment with your overall business objectives and goals. This may involve identifying key performance metrics, establishing performance targets, or developing a vision for success that reflects your organization's mission and values.

Develop performance metrics: Establish clear, measurable, and relevant performance metrics that can be used to assess progress and success. These metrics should be aligned with your organization's objectives and should be easily tracked and monitored over time.

Implement performance tracking and monitoring systems: Implement systems and processes to regularly track and monitor performance against established metrics. This may involve using data analytics tools, tracking key performance indicators (KPIs), or conducting periodic performance reviews.

Create recognition and reward programs: Develop and implement recognition and reward programs that acknowledge and celebrate individual and team achievements. Consider a mix of formal and informal recognition methods, financial and non-financial rewards, and tailor your programs to the unique needs and preferences of your employees.

Foster a culture of success: Actively promote a culture of success by encouraging collaboration, innovation, and continuous improvement. Provide resources and support for employee development, recognize and share best practices, and create opportunities for employees to contribute to the organization's success.

Communicate success stories: Regularly communicate your organization's success stories to stakeholders, including employees, customers, and investors. Share success stories in internal and external communications, highlight achievements on social media, and present success stories at industry events to maintain motivation and build trust.

Continuously evaluate and refine your approach: Regularly evaluate the effectiveness of your approach to measuring and celebrating success, and make adjustments as needed to ensure continuous improvement. Gather feedback from employees, customers, and other stakeholders, and use this information to refine your performance metrics, recognition programs, and communication strategies.

Measuring and celebrating success is vital for businesses to maintain motivation, drive performance, and create a culture of achievement. By establishing clear performance metrics, regularly reviewing progress, and acknowledging and rewarding accomplishments, organizations can foster a sense of pride and ownership in their work, improve employee retention, and enhance stakeholder confidence. Implementing the strategies discussed in this chapter can help businesses navigate the complexities of measuring and celebrating success, harness the power of achievement, and achieve lasting success in today's dynamic business environment.

www.ingramcontent.com/pod-product-compliance
Lightning Source LLC
Chambersburg PA
CBHW071550200326
41519CB00021BB/6677